Hell

CW00421036

over the Philippine Deep

Hellcats over the Philippine Deep

by

Cdr. John F. Smith, USNR (Ret.)

Sunflower University Press®
1531 Yuma (Box 1009), Manhattan, Kansas 66502-4228 USA

© 1995 by John F. Smith
Printed in the United States of America on acid-free paper.

ISBN 0-89745-182-1

All photographs from U.S. Navy sources unless otherwise noted.

Edited by Julie Bush

Layout by Lori L. Daniel

Pro Patria Mori

These are the men of Air Group 60 who will live in the hearts of their shipmates. While they lived, they lived with all their might and shared with their comrades the joy of living; mightily they died, for their air group, for their ship, and for all men.

Ensign William Bannister, *Naval Aviator*
William Barlow, *Aviation Radioman, Third Class*
Frank Barnard, *Aviation Radioman, Second Class*
Philip Barton, *Aviation Radioman, Second Class*
Lieutenant Fred Beidelman, *Naval Aviator*
John Frank Belo, *Aviation Radioman, Third Class*
Ensign Byron Brooks, *Naval Aviator*
Arnold Joe Delmenico, *Aviation Machinist Mate, Second Class*
Joseph Fina, *Aviation Machinist Mate, First Class*
Ensign Pierre Gelpi, *Naval Aviator*
Edward Harrington, *Aviation Metalsmith, First Class*
Lieutenant (jg) Earl Helwig, *Naval Aviator*
Lieutenant (jg) Paul Higginbotham, *Naval Aviator*
Ensign Charles Lamb, *Naval Aviator*
Gordon Lowrey, *Aviation Ordnanceman, Second Class*
Ralph Miller, *Aviation Radioman, Second Class*
Charles Oleson, *Aviation Radioman, Third Class*
William Proctor, *Aviation Radioman, Second Class*
Donald Rondy, *Aviation Radioman, Second Class*
Ensign William Sackrider, *Naval Aviator*
George Saladonis, *Aviation Ordnanceman, Second Class*
Bryandt Sanders, *Aviation Machinist Mate, First Class*
Peter Schwendeman, *Aviation Machinist Mate, First Class*
Lieutenant (jg) John Simpson, *Naval Aviator*
Lieutenant Byron Strong, *Naval Aviator*
Thomas Turner, *Aviation Chief Radioman*
Ernest West, *Aviation Chief Ordnanceman*
Robert Wolfe, *Aviation Ordnanceman, Second Class*

Respectfully dedicated to my comrades in Air Group 60 and to my shipmates aboard the USS ***Suwannee*** *who made the trip to the South Pacific only one way.*

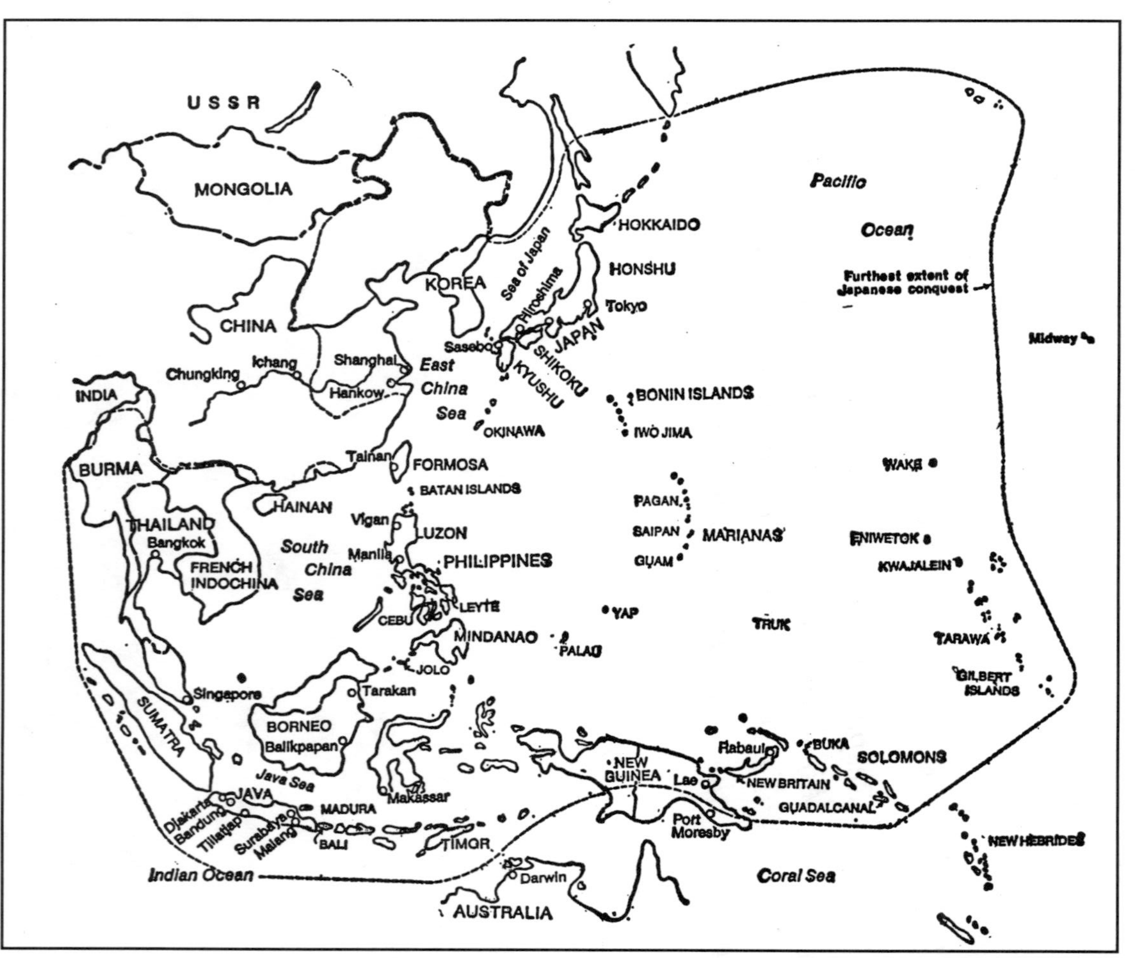

Sketch of the combat area for the Pacific war with the dashed lines showing the extreme limit of Japanese expansion before they were pushed back. This area is roughly 8 times the area of the contiguous 48 states.

Contents

Foreword

I served with John F. Smith from the time he reported to VF 60 in December 1943 until the end of the war. He was a skillful pilot and demonstrated the courage we so much appreciate on many occasions.

Most people in America during World War II knew about the Navy's combat carrier pilots. They heard often of those young men who flew off the big fast carriers, engaged in daring raids on Japanese strong points, and became involved in great air battles with Japanese aviators. Not much was said, however, about those pilots who flew off the escort carriers — the CVEs — nor has much been written.

This book is interesting and quite true to life. It tells of the CVE and its pilots, from the pilots' point of view, in a story that will be a reading pleasure for us who served on these ships during World War II; and it will enlighten those who have not had the opportunity to learn about this part of the Navy's war.

The story of the Navy during World War II is now more fully told.

Captain Royce A. Singleton, USNR (Ret.)

Acknowledgments

VERY few factual books are written solely on the basis of the author's own volition and knowledge without input from others. A number of people contributed in one way or another to the existence of the present volume. I am particularly indebted to my daughter, Letitia Ann Harder, and my son, Mark Francis Smith, for the stimuli that led to writing the original manuscript. Deep gratitude is also extended to Dominick and Ann Pellegreno for critical evaluations of the book in its original form; these led to significant revisions and, hopefully, improvement.

Thanks are also due to Londell Mannes, formerly of Iowa State University Press, for his encouragement and assistance in finding a publisher, and to Dennis Sailsbury for printing a collection of photographic negatives that were obtained from the National Archives.

Finally, the generous contributions of time and interest by Captain Royce Singleton that were necessary for him to write the Foreword is gratefully acknowledged.

The author's flight during operational training, Jacksonville Command at the Naval Air Auxiliary Field at St. Augustine, FL, 1943. Standing, left to right: Faath, Reed, Instructor Kenton. Kneeling, left to right: Carlson, Smith, Smolen. Aircraft: Grumman F4F Wildcat.

Prologue

THIS book is about a group of young men who were involved in the carrier war in the Pacific theater during World War II. These men flew F6F Hellcats in the Navy's Fighting Squadron 60 (VF 60); their average age at the time was somewhere between 21 and 23. VF 60, part of Air Group 60, served during late 1943 and all of 1944 aboard the aircraft carrier USS *Suwannee*. Air Group 60, with the ship's company of the USS *Suwannee*, was destined to be part of carrier division CarDiv 22 that converged with the newly organized Japanese kamikaze corps over the Philippine Deep in October 1944. They were the first U.S. ships to undergo such suicide attacks, which occurred in the Battle of Leyte Gulf during the invasion of the Philippines, the greatest naval battle in world history.

Information from a diversity of published references, noted in parentheses, is combined with my own experiences, as well as of other pilots and aircrew of Air Group 60. There was no intent to produce an academic history or complete record but rather to retain historical accuracy while recounting the tales of these men who were taken from a stable, peacetime environment into an active theater of a very large war. Individual anecdotes have been used to illustrate the day-to-day life in the training and development of a carrier pilot of that period.

Ships' crews have a reputation for developing a loyalty and affection for their ship, and this is certainly true for carrier pilots. It is a comforting feeling to return to the rendezvous point to find a floating home ready to receive you so that once again you avoid swimming in the briny deep. A partial list of the more important "braggin' rights" of the USS *Suwannee* include:

1. She earned 14 Official Battle Stars.
2. She twice received Presidential Unit Citations, one in conjunction with Air Group 60.
3. She participated in the first landing of American forces at Casablanca, Africa, and the last landing of American forces at Balikpapen, Borneo, plus almost every major landing in the Pacific. The total landings that she supported is greater than that of any other carrier ever built.
4. She was in the Pacific Combat Area during World War II longer than any other carrier.
5. She and her Air Group 27 share with the battleship USS *Massachusetts* credit for sinking the Vichy French battleship *Jean Bart*.
6. She was the first CVE — escort carrier — to sink an enemy submarine, a Vichy French vessel, off the African Coast. Later, in June 1944, Gene Sabin and his crew in a *Suwannee* torpedo bomber sank a Japanese submarine during the Marianas campaign. She is thus the first carrier — and one of the few — to sink submarines in both the Atlantic and Pacific theaters of operation.
7. She holds the record for being repaired in the shortest period of time after suffering severe battle damage.
8. She is believed to be the fourth leading U.S. Navy ship in terms of personnel killed in action. This is a record that survivors do not relish.
9. Her Air Group 60 was the first to use Hellcat fighters in a dive-bomber role. This became standard fleet practice and was an innovation introduced by Lieutenant Commander Harvey Feilbach, commander of VF 60.
10. Her Lieutenant Commander Feilbach developed a gun sight

that evolved into the "heads-up" display that is in use on current fighters.

11. During her operations she crossed the equator 54 times and the international date line 12 times. One of such crossings was at the intersection of these two lines and occurred during the vernal equinox with the sun simultaneously passing over the same coordinates.
12. With a logged 85 days, she holds the record for time underway under constant combat conditions. She holds second place for the record for time under way but not constantly exposed to combat conditions.
13. She was one of the few ships to enter Nagasaki harbor within weeks of the atomic bomb.
14. She participated in the largest, and generally considered greatest, naval engagement ever fought — the Battle of Leyte Gulf — where her Air Group 60 played a significant role in the amphibious landings, contributed to the sinking and damaging of many Japanese combat ships, and downed its share of enemy aircraft.

USS *Suwannee,* CVE 27.

Chapter 1

Background

World War II Combat Carrier Functions

COMBAT carrier warfare for U.S. aircraft carriers during World War II can be divided into three types. First was the warfare practiced by the fleet-type carriers, those capable of speeds of 30 knots or more that made the fast hit-and-run raids on widely separated Japanese installations. The fast carriers were, for the most part, the major participants in the sea battles between fleets; their aircraft carried the war to the enemy fleet. In contrast to naval battles in earlier wars, surface-to-surface exchange of fire was the exception rather than the rule. Surface action between Allied and Japanese cruisers off Savo Island in the Solomons was such an exception, and an outstanding exception occurred at the Battle of Leyte Gulf, where small converted carriers were indispensable.

At the start of the war, only seven U.S. fleet-class carriers were operational, with six of these — the USS *Saratoga*, USS *Lexington*, USS *Wasp*, USS *Hornet*, USS *Enterprise*, and USS *Yorktown* — in the Pacific (Fahey, 7-9). The seventh, the USS *Ranger*, was the smallest and slowest and was in the Atlantic. She put in a later period of service in the Pacific, mostly involving training duties and aircraft transport. Of the six carriers initially in the Pacific, only the USS *Saratoga* survived the war. These fleet carriers, called CVs, ranged in length from 739 to 888 feet. (In 1922, the U.S. Navy decided on an aircraft designation system: V = airplanes [heavier than air] and Z = airships [lighter than air]. Thus, the V in such ship designations as CV, CVE, and ACV indicates that they carried aircraft.)

When the Japanese bombed Pearl Harbor, 11 more large fleet carriers were under construction. These and more were completed and saw service during the war. A number of other hulls that had been laid down as cruisers were converted during construction to accept flight decks approximately 500 feet in length. These ships, fast enough to keep up with the CVs of the battle fleet, were designated as CVLs.

The nature of the fast carrier operations gave their pilots access to previously undamaged enemy installations and aircraft, generally with the element of surprise. Extensive damage was, therefore, possible, though the dangers were also formidable. Impressive results were often achieved, which led to the fast fleet carriers getting most of the press coverage and left the view in the public mind that the fast fleet carrier war was representative of the day-to-day work of all carrier pilots. Indeed, ignored in a number of histories of World War II carrier warfare was the existence of the small escort carriers, designated as CVEs. Records indicate that 85 CVEs were commissioned in the U.S. Navy during World War II. These were, at least initially, converted merchantmen. Numerically, the majority of wartime Navy pilots were engaged at one time or another flying from these small ships in the performance of the second and third type carrier functions.

The second and extremely important type of carrier warfare during World War II was against U-boats (submarines) by the convoy escorts in the North Atlantic. Convoy duty was done predominantly by small carriers. Actually, the first carrier escort of a convoy occurred in September 1942 and involved the British auxiliary carrier *Audacity* (an ex-German merchantman) equipped with old Swordfish biplane torpedo bombers (Frank, 143, 162-164). The first enemy U-boat to be sunk by an escort carrier (CVE) was a Vichy French submarine by the USS *Suwannee* off the Atlantic coast of North Africa during the Allied landings at Casablanca in November 1942 during OPERATION TORCH. By the spring of 1943, the convoy routes had air cover from shore to shore from a combination of long-range shore-based patrol planes and escort carrier aircraft.

In 1943, German U-boat losses rose from 19 boats in February and 15 in

March to 38 in May, which represented over 30 percent of the boats at sea, or nearly one in three boats that set sail. Two-thirds of these May losses resulted from air attack without contact between U-boat and convoy. The most spectacular event during the convoy war in the Atlantic was the capture of a German submarine, U-505, by the crew of a CVE commanded by then Captain (later Admiral) Dan Gallery. This U-boat is now displayed at the Museum of Science and Industry in Chicago. The story of convoy operations by CVEs in the Atlantic is well told in Y'Blood's book *Hunter-Killer*.

One of the first CVEs that had been converted from a merchantship was the USS *Long Island* (CVE 1). She was acquired by the Navy in March 1941 and commissioned the following June. Her overall length was only 492 feet, and because of truncation both fore and aft, her flight deck was only a little over 400 feet. She made a lowly maximum of 16.5 knots and had a single elevator for transporting planes back and forth between the flight and hangar decks. The small carriers were used in a variety of roles as their designations indicate: changed several times from APV (Transport and Aircraft Ferry) to AVG (Aircraft Tender, General Purpose) to ACV (Auxiliary Aircraft Carrier), and finally CVE (Aircraft Carrier Escort). The *Long Island* was followed by other conversions, several of which were released to England. Most of those that were retained by the U.S. Navy were considered to be *Bogue* class, after the USS *Bogue* (CVE 9). The exceptions were four converted oilers that made up the *Sangamon* class; these were the CVEs of largest size. A later *Casablanca* class was designed and built from the keel up as carriers; these were popularly known in the fleet as Kaiser Jeeps. A final *Commencement Bay* class was also designed from the keel up as carriers with the design being derived from the success of the *Sangamon*-class ships.

The third type of carrier warfare was close-air support of amphibious landing operations, which also involved CVEs. I have included extensive descriptions of such operations by Air Group 60 flying from CVE 27, USS *Suwannee*, during late 1943 through 1944. This period saw close-air support by the *Suwannee's* planes at a succession of amphibious landings at locations scattered over an area of approximately three million square miles. The *Suwannee*, USS *Sangamon*, and USS *Chenango* made up carrier division CarDiv 22, which was the first group of carriers to undergo kamikaze attack. The *Suwannee* was hit by kamikazes on two successive days with an additional bomb impact after the second attack, which caused enough damage to nullify operational capability until yard repairs could be made.

USS *Suwannee*, CVE 27.

The *Suwannee* and the Situation in the Pacific

A detailed history of the USS *Suwannee* has been compiled by W. R. Dacus and E. Kitzman in *As We Lived It*. The ship was originally constructed as the Standard Oil tanker *Margay* but was later acquired by the U.S. Navy with the intention of using her as a tanker. The need for carriers altered the Navy's plans, thus she and three nearly identical sister ships were given flight decks and other appropriate modifications, becoming the *Sangamon*, *Suwannee*, *Chenango*, and *Santee*. Together they constituted the *Sangamon* class of carriers and became CVEs 26 through 29. Preston, in his 1979 book *Aircraft Carriers*, has commented that these were the first truly successful conversions (137). This is attested to by the fact that their performance in the Pacific led to the laying down of keels for the construction of a whole new class of tanker-carriers, the *Commencement Bay* class. Between November 1944 and July 1946 a total of 19 were commissioned with five seeing action in the Pacific theater during 1945 (Y'Blood, Appendix).

The flight deck of the *Suwannee* was 506 feet in length, 85 feet in width, and approximately 75 feet above the waterline. The forecastle and fan tail extended, respectively, fore and aft from under the flight deck to provide an overall length of 556 feet, decreasing to 525 feet at the waterline. Under normal load she drew about 32 feet of water for a total displacement of 12,000 tons. Her oil bunkers carried 5,880 tons of fuel oil, adequate both for her and her escorting destroyers for several weeks of cruising. However, she had storage for only 100,000 gallons of aviation fuel (AvGas). She also had limited ammunition space. Air Group 60 later proved that they could exhaust her supply of 100-octane AvGas in three days of heavy operation, and the ammo magazines could be depleted in a comparable period of time.

On the *Sangamon*-class carriers, two elevators were used to bring planes back and forth between the decks. The forward elevator was just abreast the island, the superstructure on the starboard (right) side of the ship. The bridge, from which the ship was conned — piloted — was located atop the island. Above the bridge towered the mast for the signal hoists and the radio and radar antennae. In the island below the bridge was the wheel used by the quartermasters to steer the ship. The rear, or after, elevator was approximately two-thirds of the way back along the flight deck in the landing area.

A compressed-air catapult was located along the forward port (left) bow. The catapult could accelerate a fully loaded Grumman F6F Hellcat fighter or General Motors TBM Avenger torpedo bomber to flight speed in something less than 90 feet. Throughout this period, the *Sangamon, Suwannee*,

An F6F Hellcat with folded wings on deck. (Photo, Grumman Corp.)

and *Chenango* were the only CVEs to be assigned operational squadrons of F6F Hellcats; fighter squadrons on other CVEs were equipped with FM Wildcats. Nine arresting cables (commonly called wires) ran transversely across the after portion of the flight deck. During landing operations, each arresting cable was raised five or six inches above the deck by three lifters per cable. These were spaced symmetrically athwart the deck. The arresting cables operated against hydraulic dampers that rapidly decelerated a landing aircraft after its tail hook caught the cable. Hydraulic tension was controlled by crewmen in the catwalks below the deck along the side of the ship. The farther forward that a plane engaged a cable, the more rapidly it was decelerated. Memory indicates that, during an average landing, an F6F was stopped in approximately 44 feet after engaging a cable. Because such deceleration of a landing aircraft is significant, a pilot was well advised to have his shoulder harness tight and locked.

Forward of the arresting cables were a series of three barriers. Each consisted of a set of vertically spaced cables that were raised several feet into the air with the purpose of entangling an unarrested aircraft to keep it from impacting anything on the forward end of the flight deck. The last two arresting wires were in sufficiently close proximity to the barriers that, if a plane caught one of those two wires, it would impact the first and/or second barrier. However, if the plane was safely hooked, one or more of the barriers could be rapidly dropped to prevent damage. This called for rapid decision-making by the air officer on the bridge.

The USS *Suwannee* was commissioned as a carrier at Newport News, Virginia, in September 1942 under the command of Captain (later Admiral) J. J. "Jocko" Clark. After commissioning, her shakedown cruise — the initial test of the ship's performance and operation — was a trip to Africa via Bermuda to support OPERATION TORCH, the amphibious landing at Casablanca with troop landings on 8 November 1942. She carried 39 airplanes, an unprecedented load for an operational CVE. She was in company with the *Ranger, Sangamon*, and *Santee*; the *Chenango* was also present in the non-operational role of aircraft ferry with a load of 70 Curtiss P-40 Warhawks. During this operation, the *Suwannee* became the first CVE to sink a submarine, and her planes shared credit with the USS *Massachusetts* for sinking the German-manned French battleship *Jean Bart* (*Suwannee Press News*). After completion of the landings, the *Suwannee* was ordered to duty in the Pacific. En route, she passed through the Panama Canal during December 1942.

In the Pacific, the Japanese had continued to expand after their attack on

Pearl Harbor on 7 December 1941. By mid-1942, their perimeter included all of the Malay Peninsula, all of the Dutch East Indies, and the northern half of New Guinea; it went through the Solomons including the island of Guadalcanal at the southernmost point, circled north and east encompassing the Gilbert Islands, went north to the island of Kiska in the Aleutians, and finally headed back west to the Japanese home islands. The east-west distance between this bounding perimeter exceeds 5,000 statute miles, and the north-south distance exceeds 4,000 statute miles. This tremendous area is predominantly water. In addition to the war in the Pacific, though, the United States was involved in the war in Europe, and it drained the major portion of the supplies and equipment that were produced during 1942. As a result, 1942 was primarily a year for holding actions in the Pacific. Exceptions were the Battle of the Coral Sea in May, where Japanese and American carrier losses were essentially equal, and the Battle of Midway in June, which was a decisive American victory with the Japanese losing four carriers to the Americans' one.

By the beginning of 1943, however, there were enough men and materiel in the Pacific to begin to reverse the situation. Fighting on Guadalcanal was prolonged, lasting from the initial landing in early August of 1942 until the island was considered secured in late February 1943. Air Group 27 from the *Suwannee* was one among several air groups that were at one time or another based at Henderson Field on Guadalcanal to fly combat missions from there. In January of 1943, the *Suwannee* also participated by providing close-air support for an amphibious landing on Renell Island. Her Air Group 27 was active throughout the northwestern movement of the Allies through the Solomons group. This activity included engagements at the Russells, Bougainville, New Georgia, Rendova, and Vangunu. In August 1943, she was ordered back to the San Francisco Bay area for yard work and for the replacement of her Air Group 27 by Air Group 60.

By the fall of 1943, availability of men and materiel had built to the point where extensive operations could be launched against the Japanese in the Pacific. General Douglas MacArthur in the Southwest Pacific was about to break out of the Solomons to commence his campaign across the northern coast of New Guinea to Morotai in the Dutch East Indies and thence north to the Philippines, with the ultimate goal being the Japanese homeland. Simultaneously, the Navy under Admiral Chester Nimitz's command was about to undertake an island-hopping campaign across the Central Pacific. This campaign was to be spearheaded by the Marine divisions. As a result, in October 1943 the *Suwannee* found herself moored to a dock at the Naval

Air Station in San Diego, and Air Group 60 came aboard. *Suwannee* was fresh from the yard after completion of some refitting, and Air Group 60 had just completed its training.

The Air Group

What was to become Air Group 60 was born on a cold, wintry day in early 1943. The incident is described in the yearbook, published after the group's return to the United States in December 1944, whose costs were borne by Captain W. D. Johnson, then skipper of the USS *Suwannee*, as a parting gift to the group. Captain Johnson was at the time still recovering from wounds suffered during the second kamikaze hit on his ship. When the air group was detached from the *Suwannee*, he requested that the pilots all stop by his convalescent quarters where he shook hands with each of the men. The yearbook notes:

> At 0900, 24 February, 1943, U.S. Naval Air Station, in Seattle, Washington, — A cold snowy morning, a morning made for better things in a sailor's life, but just the same the call went forth — a bugle call, loud and clear, sounding through the big hangar; "All hands to quarters; uniform Dress Blue Affirm." The zero temperature and rapidly falling snow made crystal patterns on the shoulders of the men as they fell in and smartly answered the call.
>
> Skippered in those days by a tall, smiling, red-headed man, Lieutenant Commander John H. Pennoyer, and squired by the leading and only CPO John W. Sousley (who has squired, nursed, profaned, and sweated over us ever since), and a motley, but promising group of twenty-one blue jackets, we were on that fateful day, brought to attention while the almighty words were pronounced: "I hereby commission you, Escort Scouting Squadron Sixty."

Between February and May the addition of planes and personnel brought the squadron to full complement and the designation was changed to VC 60, indicating a composite squadron — one made up of many added elements. On 7 May the squadron moved to Astoria, Oregon, where flying was in accord with a training syllabus. On 15 July another change in designation made the squadron an air group. As part of the redesignation ceremony,

Distinguished Flying Crosses were pinned to the breast of Lieutenant Fred "Bugs" Beidelman, for having sunk a Japanese destroyer during the Battle of the Solomons the previous fall, and to the breast of Chief Radioman Red Turner, for bagging two Japanese Mitsubishi A6M Zero fighters from the rear seat of an SBD Dauntless dive-bomber during that same battle. These two heroes were destined later to die on consecutive days during kamikaze attacks in the Battle of Leyte Gulf. The designation of air group was a result of the addition in early August of several dive-bombers and crews under the command of Lieutenant W. C. "Butch" Vincent and the redesignation of the fighters as fighter squadron VF 60. The complete group thus included VF 60 flying 12 Grumman F6F Hellcats and a composite squadron, VC 60, flying 9 General Motors TBM Avenger torpedo bombers (Grumman's version was the TBF) and 9 Douglas SBD Dauntless scout dive-bombers.

Shortly thereafter, the fighter and torpedo portions of the air group were detached to Holtville, California, in the Imperial Valley near the Mexican border. Extensive night training was undertaken. Two VF pilots were lost in fatal accidents during that period; one, Junior Brooks, crashed during a night strafing exercise, and his replacement, Pierre Gelpi, apparently lost consciousness and crashed due to hypoxia during a night high-altitude flight. A third, less tragic accident also occurred during that time and resulted in a lasting nickname. The details of what led to the crash landing are not important, but Herman Walters, one of several Texans in the squadron, found himself in a wrecked F6F alone in the dark desert. The squadron flew through the rest of the night in vain attempts to locate him. In the meantime, Walters had extricated himself from his bent bird and had walked 14 miles through the sand of the rattlesnake-infested desert to arrive at the station's medical dispensary in time for breakfast. From then on he was known as "Fearless Fosdick" after the character in Al Capp's cartoon *Li'l Abner*.

After night training, the fighter and torpedo crews were ordered to Los Alamitos, just south of Los Angeles, where they rejoined the dive-bomber crews. Then in mid-September the torpedo crews flew to San Diego where they were able to drop some practice torpedoes. This practice was to stand them in good stead when they dropped live ones 13 months later. The ample spare time at Los Alamitos was spent partying and interacting with females of the species. Unfortunately, all good things must end, and the squadrons were ordered to San Diego to board the USS *Suwannee* on 16 October 1943. By 18 October, all personnel and equipment were on board, and the ship put to sea the next day with Point Loma disappearing below the stern later in the morning.

Japanese Special Attack Corps

In addition to the *Suwannee* and Air Group 60, the third member of the triumvirate that converged over the Philippine Deep in October 1944 was the Japanese kamikaze corps. Formation of this corps had resulted from the extent of Japanese losses of trained combat pilots. Such losses were particularly severe at the Battle of Midway in June 1942 and during the battle west of the Marianas in June 1944 in what has come to be called the Battle of the Philippine Sea, but which was known to U.S. Naval Aviators of the time as the "Marianas Turkey Shoot." The extent of the losses placed Japanese naval air power in a markedly inferior position relative to U.S. air power; losses elsewhere had similarly affected their army air power. At the beginning of the war, the Japanese Zero (Allied code-named "Zeke") was the premier fighter in the Pacific theater. It was faster and more maneuverable than its Allied counterparts. But by mid-1943, this was no longer the case; the Zero was surpassed in both speed and stamina by America's F6F Hellcat, F4U Corsair, and P-38 Lightning.

As early as July 1944, the idea of a Japanese suicide corps was proposed in a letter to his superiors by Captain Eiichiro Jyo, who then commanded the light carrier *Chiyoda*:

> No longer can we hope to sink the numerically superior enemy aircraft carriers through ordinary attack methods. I urge the immediate organization of special attack units to carry out crash-dive tactics, and I ask to be placed in command of them. (Inoguchi, Nakajima, and Pineau, 29)

However, the initiation of such units did not occur until the following October.

On 17 October 1944, American ships appeared off Suluan Island at the mouth of Leyte Gulf in sufficient numbers to indicate an imminent invasion. At that time, the entire Japanese air force in the Philippines consisted of fewer than 100 operational aircraft. Also on 17 October, Admiral Takijiro Ohnishi had arrived in the Philippines to assume command of the Japanese First Air Fleet. Two days later the Admiral visited Mabalacat on the island of Luzon where the Japanese 201st Air Group was stationed under Commander Asaichi Tamai. At a meeting during that visit, Admiral Ohnishi outlined the dire situation facing the Japanese forces and indicated that the U.S. carriers should be hit and kept neutralized for at least a week. He suggested:

> In my opinion, there is only one way of assuring that our meager strength will be effective to a maximum degree. That is to organize suicide attack units composed of Zero fighters armed with 250-kilogram bombs, with each plane to crash-dive into an enemy carrier. (Inoguchi, Nakajima, and Pineau, 7)

In accord with this suggestion and after consultation with his pilots, Tamai agreed to organize such units within his air group, and on 20 October Admiral Ohnishi signed an announcement that sanctioned these units. Someone remembered Japanese history and the fact that in 1281 Kublai Khan had assembled a large fleet bent on invading and conquering Japan. During the passage toward Japan, this fleet was destroyed by a great typhoon that came to be known as the Divine Wind, and this was the name chosen for the suicide corps. The Japanese characters for "Divine Wind" can be rendered as either *shimpu* or *kamikaze*, and it is the latter name that has been used extensively for these units in the West. Although there are many instances of U.S. servicemen fighting to the death, the concept of deliberate suicide is alien to Western philosophy, and those who witnessed the kamikaze attacks found them difficult to understand.

Chapter 2

The First Operation and Other Considerations

AFTER departing San Diego, the *Suwannee* sailed south for Espiritu Santo in the New Hebrides where she dropped anchor in Segond Channel. On 2 November 1944, en route to Espiritu, the *Suwannee* had crossed the equator, and the "pollywogs" — the new members — of Air Group 60 were duly subjected to the indignities of the initiation ceremonies to become more experienced "shellbacks." The stay at Espiritu was short, and the ship and air group soon moved approximately 130 nautical miles to the southwest to Efate, still in the New Hebrides. There AG 60 practiced for its first operation, which was to be a support unit for the upcoming Marine invasion of the Japanese-held Tarawa and Makin atolls in the Gilberts.

Lieutenant Commander Allan "Ace" Edmands was commander of the VC squadron as well as of Air Group 60 when CarDiv 22, commanded by Rear Admiral V. H. Ragsdale and a unit of Task Force 53 under Rear Admiral Harry Hill, was deployed on 13 November to Tarawa. In addition to the three converted oilers, the *Sangamon, Suwannee*, and *Chenango*, two *Bogue*-class carriers were added to CarDiv 22 for this operation, the *Barnes* and the

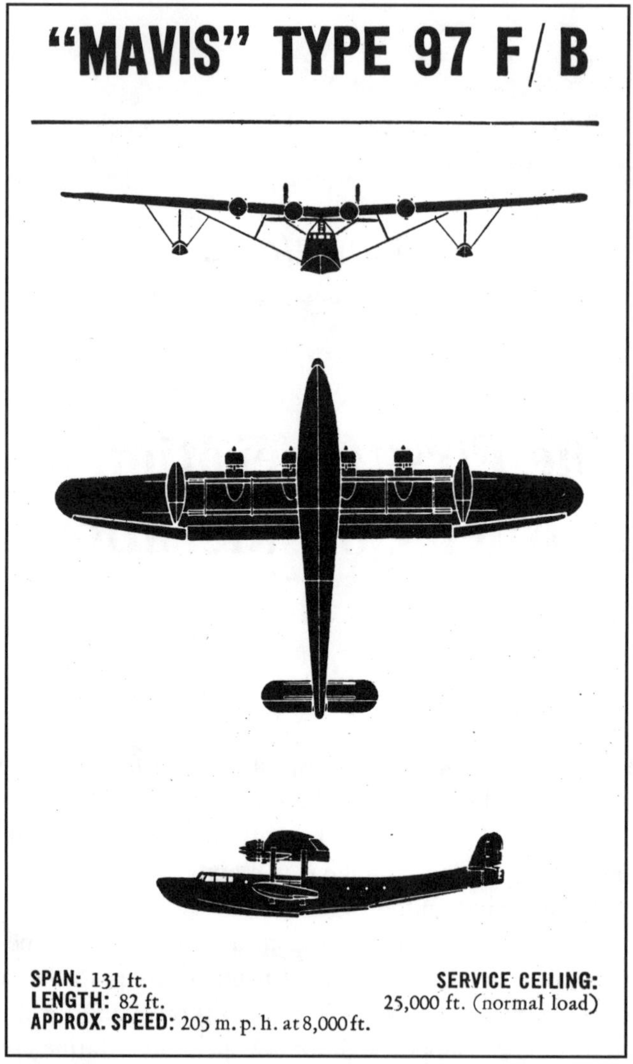

(*Recognition Pictorial Manual*, War Dept. FM 30-30, Navy Dept. Bauer 3, 1943)

Nassau, and their function was to serve as ferries for the Hellcats of VF 1, the Navy's garrison squadron scheduled to be left on Tarawa after its capture. Though it had not been planned to use these latter two carriers in an operational role, developments during the operation caused them to be pressed into service.

Kawanishi H6K5 patrol bomber. Code Name: Mavis; four 900 hp engines; wingspan: 131 ft, 4 in.; gross wt: 45,000 lbs. (*Recognition Pictorial Manual*)

Anticipating new experiences involving danger and excitement, Air Group 60 moved north. During the trip, destroyers in the screen — a peripheral deployment of smaller, faster ships, usually destroyers or destroyer escorts, whose function is to protect the primary fleet — reported a number of sonic contacts, but it was never confirmed nor refuted that these represented actual submarines. Radar responses from aircraft were also received on two occasions. In the first instance, no contact was made, but when the second radar blip appeared, it was a different story. Lieutenant Ed "Dash" Dashiell was at the time leading the combat air patrol (CAP) above the carriers. His flight was vectored to intercept the enemy — the "bogey." Contact was made and the bogey proved to be a four-engine Japanese Kawanishi flying boat code-named "Mavis." Dash and his wingman, Winston "Gun" Gunnels, promptly dispatched the Mavis, and first blood was drawn by the air group. Indeed, this was done so efficiently that pilots in the second section, John "Rabbi" Shea and Givens "Cess" Wilson, didn't have the opportunity to fire a shot. It is believed that the Mavis was on a long-range patrol and its crew mistook the American aircraft for shore-based Japanese aircraft, because the Americans were receiving blinker-light signals from the Mavis as they were making their gunnery pass. Analysis of the event aboard the ship led to the conclusion that there was little likelihood that the Mavis had sent out a radio warning of the American presence in the area.

Pre-landing strikes began before dawn on the morning of D-day, 20 November 1943. Air Group 60's efforts were directed at Betio, an islet on the south side of the Tarawa atoll in the Gilbert Islands. Tarawa was formidably fortified and capable of heavy antiaircraft fire. Hank Carey in an F6F and Jud Lavin in a TBM both received wing damage from this fire.

Operational accidents were also common during this operation, largely due to weak prevailing winds that combined with the slow carrier speed to produce very low wind velocities over the flight deck. Such low wind velocities made both launching and recovery of aircraft particularly hazardous. During this Gilbert operation, two F6Fs turned turtle and wound up on their backs on the flight deck. The first, which involved Quinn "Frog" La Fargue, resulted in no injuries, but in the second, which involved Ed "Fish" Fischer, two plane handlers on deck were injured — one received a broken leg and the other a skull fracture.

On 20 November, four TBMs fell in the water; these were piloted by Ace Edmands, Joe Bacon, Jud Lavin, and Glen "Okie" Banks. Banks's accident was the most serious and led to the only fatality of the operation. During a takeoff in a heavily loaded TBM, he failed to obtain adequate airspeed and mushed into the water. As the crew was exiting the airplane, one or more of its load of depth charges exploded. Banks's leg was broken in several places, and he was taken aboard a destroyer and then evacuated to a shore hospital. The gunner was blown into the air but was otherwise unhurt and returned aboard the *Suwannee*. Unfortunately, the radioman, Johnny Belo, was killed and never made it out of the airplane.

Japanese submarines operated in the area, and one of them, the *I-175*, put two torpedoes into the *Casablanca*-class CVE the *Liscome Bay*. At the time, the *Liscome Bay* was operating off Makin, the second landing site in the Gilberts. The torpedo hits ruptured a gasoline storage bunker and leaking gasoline caught fire, which engendered a violent explosion. After only 23 minutes the *Liscome Bay* vanished beneath the waves. On another occasion, two U.S. destroyers, the *Meade* and the *Frazier*, caught the Japanese *I-35*, and their depth charging brought the submarine to the surface where the *Frazier* rammed her. As the submarine sank, *Suwannee* TBMs rained depth charges on her. Both the *Meade* and the *Frazier* launched whale boats to pick up survivors. However, a TBM pilot mistook the *Meade's* whale boat for a Japanese submarine's conning tower and forthwith dropped a bomb near the boat. When it exploded, it lifted the boat clear off the water and caused the crew to go swimming. The *Meade* in turn took the bombing as indicative that the airplane was Japanese and promptly opened fire, scoring two hits before recognizing the plane as friendly. The TBM pilot also recognized his mistake and promptly departed the area. Fortunately, there were no personnel injuries on either side.

After operating off Tarawa from 20 November to 14 December 1944, the three *Sangamons* were detached to San Diego with a stop at Pearl Harbor en route. At Pearl Harbor, all remaining planes and useful materiel were transferred ashore. But before departure from the Tarawa area, four pilots — Hank Carey and Winston Gunnels from VF and Jud Lavin and Joe Bacon from VC — and crews from the *Suwannee* were tranferred to the fast carrier CVL squadrons to replace losses that had been incurred. The transfer of these pilots generated the need for replacements.

Most of the pilots who later joined VF 60 were at the time of the Gilbert invasions in the terminal phases of their flight training. The training of a Naval Aviator of that period progressed through preflight school (primarily physical conditioning), primary training, basic training, instrument training, and finally more specialized advanced training. After advanced training (also known as final squadron), an Aviation Cadet was commissioned and assigned to any one of a variety of billets, such as operational training (for those soon to be sent to the fleet), the ferry command, landing signal officer training, photo school, and the like. The only ones who were assigned directly to operating squadrons immediately after commissioning were patrol-plane pilots to patrol squadrons, multi-engine pilots to the transport command, or float-plane pilots to in-shore patrol or to a cruiser or battleship. It normally took about nine months from completion of preflight school to commissioning.

Because of the need for pilots, the flight schedules were heavy with congested flying, frequently in less than ideal weather. As a result, operational accidents were not uncommon, with the percentage of fatalites increasing with the level of sophistication of the training. The accident rate tended to decrease with the passage of time as the students' skills improved. This correlates with the "wash out" or elimination rate, which was highest in primary and lowest in advanced squadron.

In primary training, whole squadrons were scheduled to take off or land at approximately the same time, resulting in periods of high congestion. Any cadet of that period could recount a number of hair-raising experiences. I observed one incident while at Naval Air Station (NAS) Glenview, Illinois, for carrier qualification. Glenview also served as a primary training base. At the end of a one-hour training period, Stearman N2S Kaydet planes of the training squadrons would come flocking back to base like grackles to a roost. On one particular day, the planes were returning, and a group of eight to ten of them were observed on simultaneous final approach. Two young gentlemen pilots were obviously concentrating on making good landings and neglected to look out for other airplanes. One drifted left and the other right, leading to a gentle caress of their outer wing panels with subsequent, very unwinglike distortion. The two planes fluttered relatively gently to earth, and fortunately, neither pilot was injured, but the squadron operations officer undoubtedly made known to them that he was not pleased with their performance.

Minor accidents of various types, particularly ground loops, were typical of primary training. During the three months that I was in primary at Norman, Oklahoma, there were only one or two fatalities at the station. In comparison, in operational training at Green Cove Springs, Florida, where each flight consisted of seven students and an instructor, they were averaging one fatality per six flights or one every 3,600 hours of flight time. This level was still in effect when a number of VF 60 pilots were assigned as instructors to the operational training command after the squadron's return to the States in December 1944.

I observed such a fatality while flying F4F Wildcats during operational training in Florida. The student pilot was Affie Pearce, a friendly bear of a man who was exceedingly proud of his partial Seminole Indian heritage. On one occasion, while over the ocean, he had an engine stoppage due to a vapor lock during a high-G pullout from an overhead gunnery run. He had handled the situation calmly and correctly and had restarted the engine before splashing. A few days later, the flight was again scheduled for an over-water gunnery hop; pilots were wearing inflatable life jackets. Takeoffs were toward a broad, sweeping bend in Florida's St. John's River and were in sequence. Shortly after his takeoff, Affie's engine again quit. Instead of continuing forward to ditch in the river, he tried to turn back to the field. In the process, he lost speed and spun into the ground. Watching the event during takeoff roll left an empty feeling in the pit of my stomach.

Some unusual incidents were, in retrospect, actually funny. During primary training, in aerobatic stage, I was assigned to do aerobatics during a one-hour solo hop. Standard doctrine was for all aerobatic maneuvers to be completed above 2,000 feet. I took off in an open-cockpit Stearman N2S and proceeded to the aerobatic area. I began with some loops, split-S's, chandelles, snap rolls, and the like, which are all exercises that impose positive G-loads to keep the pilot in his seat. I then decided to do an Immelmann, a half-loop followed by a half-roll from inverted to normal flight. I completed the half-loop and pushed forward on the stick to stabilize before rolling. At this point, and as a complete surprise to me, the airplane and I started to part company. My adrenaline flowed and my grip on the stick tightened correspondingly. I was wearing a parachute, so I wasn't worried about surviving, but I remember thinking, "How am I going to explain the loss of this airplane to the operations officer?" I found myself inverted with my feet falling free of the rudders. The only thing holding me and the airplane together was my choke-like grip on the stick.

Fortunately, the stick was securely attached, but my weight hanging vertically downward did nothing to change the attitude of the inverted ship. I maneuvered one foot to the side against a longeron — part of the aircraft's framework — and pushed. This moved me and the stick off center so that the Stearman very sloppily rolled around and let me fall back into the seat. Needless to say, I lost no time in buckling my seat belt, and I flew right-side up for most of the rest of the period to calm my nerves. To this day, I don't know whether I forgot to buckle my safety belt or whether, during the flight, the sleeve of my heavy flying jacket caught the lever that unlocked it.

Another experience during primary training, though not funny at the time, now appears humorous. It was an extremely cold day with the temperature near 0°F. Heavy wool-lined flight suits, boots, and mittens were worn. Leather face masks were available, but because they severely restricted vision, I did not wear one on this flight, even though the rear cockpit of the Stearman was much more drafty than the front. Upon return to the ready room after an hour's flight, I found that my lips had chapped to the extent that they bled. The blood had clotted and I couldn't open my mouth. A very quiet cadet was immediately sent by the instructor to sick bay where the situation was remedied.

A shortcoming of the Navy's Primary Training Program during World War II was its training for night flying. The average cadet's first time aloft in the night sky was an interesting experience. A runway was marked on the asphalt mat by flare pots. The N2S had running lights but no landing light. Traffic was controlled with a signal light known as an Aldis lamp from alongside the approach end of the runway. The student would meet his instructor at the assigned airplane, and the instructor would say something to the effect that the only difference between day flying and night flying was that you couldn't see as well at night. They would then take off into the inky black with the student instructed to observe.

The first half of the period was spent doing airwork for familiarization; the second half was for landings. The first landing would be a demonstration, the second landing was supposed to have the student follow through on the dual controls, and the third and successive landings were supposed to be made by the student with the instructor making corrections. In practice, "corrections" meant that the instructor had a vise-like grip on the controls and that any change the student wished to make would require hydraulic boost to overcome the instructor's control.

After landing and return to the flight line, the student would be informed that he had done a commendable job and was ready to go alone on the next flight into the black, starlit night. And go alone he did, but with considerable trepidation until he got the hang of night approaches and landings on his own. In retrospect, I think the problem was that the vast majority of primary instructors of that period were brought into the Navy directly from civilian aviation with little or no night flying experience in their own background, and they were given very little additional night time before being assigned to instruct at a training base. This approach to night flying seems to have persisted throughout the war. A pilot really didn't feel comfortable flying at night until after doing so in the fleet.

Either Corpus Christi, Texas, or Pensacola, Florida, was the site for basic training following primary. Basic was simply an exposure to higher horsepower, slightly more complex aircraft. The Vultee SNV Valiant was used. Instrument training was an introduction and was done either in SNVs or North American SNJ Texans with the student in the back seat under a hood. All potential carrier pilots did their advanced training in SNJs, and this was the first split for specialization with some auxiliary fields designated for fighter training, some for torpedo-bomber training, and some for dive-bomber training. Fighter training emphasized fixed gunnery on airborne sleeves — hollow fabric tubes as "targets," 30 inches in diameter and 20 feet long; instrument flight on partial panel — with some of the instruments covered; and some bombing, formation, and aerobatic practice with a mandatory demonstration of ability to recover from both normal and inverted spins. The inverted spins were done in an N3N, an airplane manufactured at the Philadelphia Naval Aircraft Factory and considered by pilots to be as strong as a tank.

A student's initial exposure to gunnery flight runs began in the rear seat while an instructor made the actual runs. Students made practice or dummy gunnery runs over a land area designated for that purpose before actual firing was done over water in an off-shore gunnery range. Glenn "Red" Rynearson of VF 60 told of an experience he had with a dummy gunnery flight at Corpus Christi. Red, who was in advanced squadron but had not yet progressed to the gunnery phase, was flying tail-end Charlie in a flight practicing formation flying. Whether the formation flight strayed south of its practice area into the gunnery range or the dummy gunnery flight strayed north into the formation practice area is something of which Red is unsure. What he is sure of is that he caught a glimpse from the corner of his eye of a plane diving past, soon followed by a second, and then a third, which hit him. It took off most of his fin and rudder, then scraped a wing across the top of his canopy and through his propeller, costing the gunnery pilot a portion of his wing and Red his means for developing thrust. The gunnery pilot bailed out immediately, but Red still had aileron control and some elevator control, so he experimented to see if he could manage the airplane sufficiently to make a dead-stick landing. However, Red decided that with little or no directional control, it was wiser to bail out.

Red landed at the headquarters of the Chapman Ranch, a part of the King complex — part of a large conglomerate that covers a major portion of southeastern Texas — and the only inhabited location for miles around. He hit a sloping roof or wall of an outbuilding and slid down onto an abutting flat roof, from which he was reluctant to jump the additional way to the ground. Apparently all the ranch hands were out on the range except for one who was too old for such work. When this old man wandered by and saw Red, he seemed puzzled by the strange gift from heaven that had been bestowed upon his roof. Communication was a problem as the ranch hand's native language seemed to be Spanish, but ultimately he did get a ladder and took Red to the main house where a lady graciously provided a telephone. The Navy came to Red's rescue to end the adventure.

For firing runs, each plane was loaded with a fixed number of rounds of ammunition, which were coated on the tips with a slow-drying paint. Each plane in a flight had a different color so that after the run, the holes in the sleeve could be counted and scored to the appropriate pilot. One plane in each gunnery flight was assigned as tow guard, and his function was to fly alongside the tow plane to and from the gunnery range to prevent an inadvertent mishap with other aircraft that might not see the tow. Actual firing was done over water with the gunnery flight streamed in trail well ahead, above, and to one side or other of the tow. Each plane in turn peeled off, charged its gun, made its run on the sleeve, and, with ordnance again on "safe" to prevent accidental firing, climbed back into position at the stern of the flight. If properly executed, no plane was ever in line of fire with another.

A variety of gunnery runs were made. Side runs were executed with the firing plane approaching the target in a diving turn from ahead and above and, ideally, reaching firing position with 70- to 90-degree deflection. It must be remembered that because of the target's relative motion, the aiming point had to be well ahead of the sleeve. A dangerous approach occurred when the timing of the approach turn was bad and the gunnery plane came into range at an angle of 30 degrees or less. At such a low angle there was a danger of hitting the tow plane, and sadly, such incidents did occur. Another danger was the possibility of getting a sleeve draped around the firing plane. This could occur in two ways: when the pilot continued firing until he was too close to avoid impact, or when the target was over-led and the tow line was shot in two. Hitting the tow was fairly benign if it draped around a wing, because the SNJ was a rugged bird and could handle this type of load. However, the sleeve could be lethal if it draped around the cockpit, which could blind the pilot, or around the aircraft's tail, which could make the controls ineffective.

Even instrument flights could have their moments of excitement. While in advanced squadron at Corpus Christi, I found myself scheduled with an instructor for such a flight. When he arrived at the assigned ship, he was in the company of another instructor, and they had their heads together in a serious discussion. I climbed into the back seat, where the hood was located, and my instructor climbed into the front and fired the engine. He looked over at another plane where his friend had also climbed aboard and had started its engine; a cadet was in the rear seat of that plane as well. The two instructors exchanged waves and both called in sequence for taxi clearance. When clear of the field, the two planes joined in formation and headed slightly southwest. I was told to sit back and relax; it wasn't going to be a working flight.

The flight was scheduled for a period of an hour and a half, and after flying slightly less than half that time, we arrived at one of the King ranches. The other plane was the lead plane, and he made an approach and landed in a pasture to the northwest of the ranch housing. We landed second and quite uneventfully. We taxied to the vicinity of the main house, and after getting out, the two instructors immediately began an animated conversation with the people from the ranch — apparently about a recent party where they had met. We two cadets were taken into the house and given cold watermelon. But because of the constraints of the flight schedule, we didn't stay long and were soon loaded back into the planes.

Our young instructor heroes decided to show the Texas aristocracy some fancy takeoffs, so they didn't bother to taxi to the far side of the pasture. Instead, they taxied to the middle of the field and took off, again in sequence rather than in formation, with a heading toward an orchard immediately west of the house. The distance actually was enough for a normal takeoff; the first plane lifted off comfortably. But my pilot was impatient and started his takeoff roll very shortly after the first plane. As a result, when we were at the position that we would normally have become airborne, we encountered a very strong downwash from the wing vortex of the first plane. This kept us on the ground and we went through a barbed-wire fence before lifting off into an orchard. I can remember looking up into the branches as we passed through, but because I was not in control, there was really nothing I could do but watch the sequence of events. I was calm but recall wondering how many acres the wreckage would cover, and if I would survive to know. Surprisingly, and to the credit of the stout construction of the SNJ, the ship remained airborne and plowed its way up through the tree branches to emerge into the clear sky.

Though I must fault the instructor for bad judgment in his takeoff procedure, I'll give him credit for his subsequent handling of the situation. He had brains enough not to retract the wheels, because they might have stuck in the up position. He also climbed to a safe altitude and checked the slow flight characteristics with and without flaps to determine what approach speed to use into the airport. We continued the flight back to base, keeping a close monitor on the oil temperature gauge and upon the fuel supply to be sure that we had not put a hole in one or the other tank. At the base the landing was uneventful, though the instructor wisely opted for a wheel landing rather than a full-stall landing. Afterward, we found a couple of long strands of barbed wire dragging from the wheel fairings, a short length of limb about one and a half inches in diameter wedged into the broken landing light, and numerous pieces of tree of assorted size distributed inside the cowling around the cylinders. The instructor filled out an accident report and told me to sign it. It stated that the mishap had occurred at field 13, which was one our practice fields, and that the instructor took full responsibility by giving me a simulated engine failure when it was too late to avoid going through the fence and trees at the end of the runway. I think that I can say I wound up only a little older but very much wiser for this experience.

Chapter 3

Movement Northwest and Invasion of Kwajalein

The Trip to the Marshalls

THREE young ensigns — Murphy, Smolen, and I — left Kansas City for Los Angeles on the evening of 22 December 1943 aboard a TWA DC3. We had just come off leave after carrier qualification on the Great Lakes and were headed for another Christmas away from home, but we were excited because we were reporting to San Diego for assignment to fleet squadrons. Murphy was a Chicago boy and was destined to serve aboard the USS *Kitkun Bay*, which received shell fire from Japanese surface units during the Battle of Leyte Gulf. This shelling occurred on the same day that CarDiv 22, including the USS *Suwannee*, encountered the kamikaze nemesis. We were due to report to the Naval Air Station at San Diego before 2400 hours — midnight — on 23 December.

Weather to the west of Wichita, Kansas, promised severe storms with turbulence and restricted visibility, so the flight was held overnight at Wichita. This led to a late arrival in Los Angeles, and the train to San Diego for which we had been scheduled was long gone. The next train arrived in San Diego near midnight, and the trip between the train station and the Naval Air Station on North Island with its ferry ride across the bay caused us to report to the Officer of the Day 40 minutes over leave. The *Sangamon* was berthed immediately adjacent to the ferry landing, so the three of us passed alongside it on our way to the OD's office. Having never seen a seagoing carrier, we thought she seemed huge, though by today's standards she was quite small. The sound of pumps, ventilators, and other strange noises of a living ship could be heard. We were awed to think that we would soon be aboard her.

During training we had been taught that being over leave in the Navy was a heinous offense. With this indoctrination, we three anticipated, at best, a severe reprimand and, at worst — our imaginations trembled. However, the OD's office at NAS San Diego was so busy that no one seemed to care whether we even showed up, much less that we had missed reporting time by some 40 minutes. The OD simply took our orders, logged them in, told us where to find sleeping quarters, and instructed us to report back at 0700. At 0700 we each were handed individual orders and were separated. I was assigning to fighter squadron VF 60 and was told to proceed to Hangar 10 where the VF 60 Duty Officer could be found. It took only a few minutes to walk to Hangar 10, and I was logged in as a member of the squadron before breakfast on Christmas Eve, a total elapsed time at NAS San Diego of less than eight hours. Such was the way assignments were made during wartime.

The *Suwannee* and *Chenango* were berthed not far from the *Sangamon*, and all air groups were temporarily ashore to replace aircraft and materiel. Also, Air Group Commander Ace Edmands was detached to other duties. There was thus a need for six replacement pilots, two VF and four VC. D. O. "Dew" Timm and I filled the VF billets left open by Hank Carey and Winston Gunnels, and Joe Delk, Hal Jedlund, Paul Higginbotham, and Bob Chase filled the VC billets vacated by Glen Banks, Joe Bacon, Jud Lavin, and Ace Edmands. Neither Timm nor I was carrier qualified in the F6F, nor for that matter was Wilbur "Willie" Schmall, who had joined the squadron too late in October to qualify before departure for the Tarawa operation. We three were worked hard during the period between Christmas and New Year's. The major portion of the flight time was devoted to field carrier landing practice (commonly known as "bounce drill"), including night landings. The landing signal officer (LSO) from the ship's company, Bob Misbach, worked with us until he was satisfied that he could bring us aboard under any

An F4F Wildcat, Grumman's first monoplane. (Photo, Grumman Corp.)

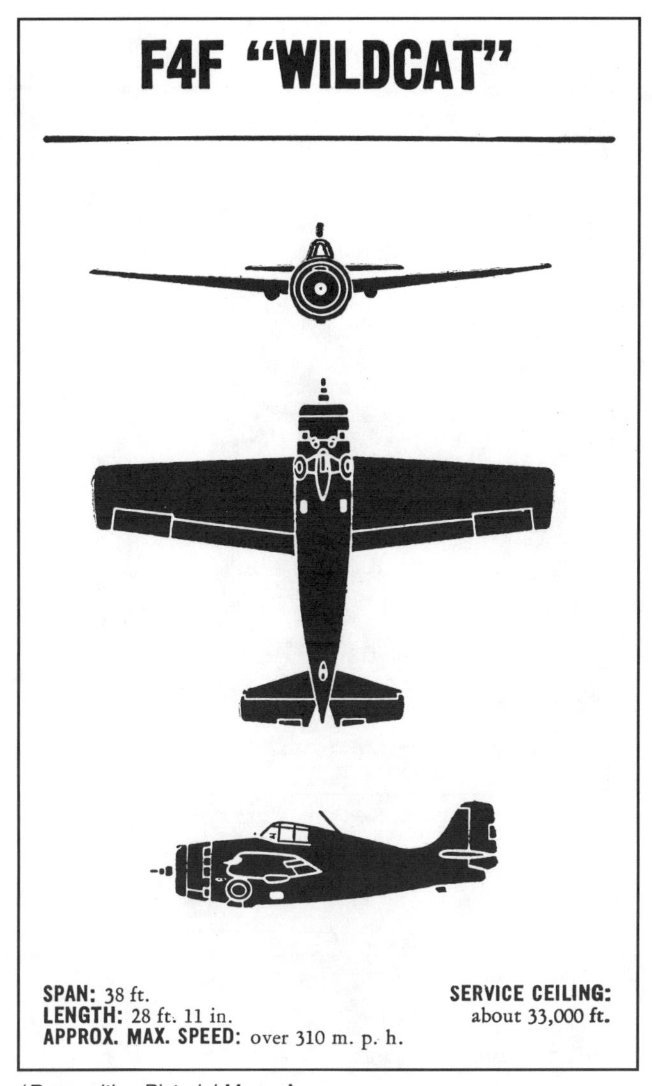

(*Recognition Pictorial Manual*)

and all conditions. Roughly 25 hours were logged before we proceeded to sea shortly after New Year's aboard the *Altamaha* for carrier qualification in the F6F.

The Grumman F6F Hellcat was a big brother to the Wildcat (the FM2, as built by General Motors, and the F4F, as built by Grumman — the plane was

The Grumman F6F Hellcat, which compiled an overall kill ratio of 19:1 during World War II combat action. (Photo, Grumman Corp.)

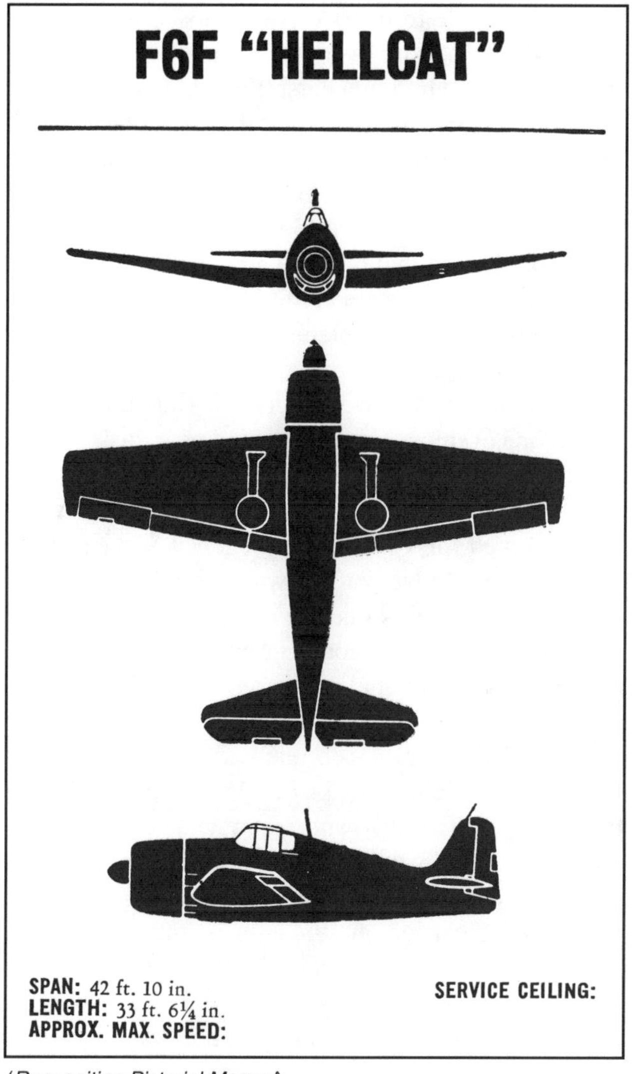

(*Recognition Pictorial Manual*)

the same but made by different manufacturers) with a wingspan of 42 feet 10 inches compared to the Wildcat's 38 feet, a gross weight of 15,400 pounds compared to the Wildcat's 7,950, and a maximum speed not quite 100 miles per hour greater (see Tillman; Swanborough and Bowers, 218). It was a low, mid-wing monoplane with 2,000 horsepower, and it used hydraulics rather than muscle to operate cowl flaps, landing gear, wing fold, and gun chargers. After logging over 750 hours in this airplane, I found no bad things to say about it; Grandma herself would have been comfortable in it. The F6F Hellcat was the right plane at the right place at the right time. Both the U.S. and British Navies thought highly of it, and between the two they contracted with the Grumman "Iron Works" to build and deliver over 12,000 F6Fs in a 30-month period during 1943 to 1945. At the end of the war, official records showed that 6,477 enemy aircraft fell to carrier aircraft of the U.S. Navy, and Hellcats were credited with 5,155 of these. VF 60 was fortunate to be equipped with this plane.

Camaraderie and morale were high in the VF 60 squadron, which was demonstrated to me during the week between Christmas and New Year's 1943. I was irked one evening when we landed near dusk and found that we were to climb almost immediately back into our airplanes for night flying. My irritation was due to the fact that I had a date with a Wave — a member of the Women Accepted for Volunteer Emergency Service. The availability of young ladies in a strictly Navy town was quite limited in wartime, and I therefore wanted to stay in this one's good graces. But there was no telephone available and I could not contact her. However, I soon learned the close-knit nature of an operational squadron. I had bleated my woes to the lads on the flight line before I took off for the scheduled night flight. As a result, when I landed they had a jeep ready to go, and three of them drove me off the base to my date's barracks on Coronado peninsula. It was well above and beyond the call of duty, and I appreciated it. The young lady forgave me for being late, and we had a good time that evening. Fortunately, I was able to repay at least one of my benefactors at a later date.

After completion of carrier qualification in the F6F, we replacements found the squadron busy getting aircraft, equipment, and personnel aboard ship. Little time was available for anything else. Loading of the aircraft was of particular interest to those who had not seen it before. Aircraft were taxied with wings folded right down to the dock alongside the carrier. A cable was let down from a hoist mounted alongside the flight deck and was attached to a fitting on the aircraft, which was lifted and swung over to be let down on deck.

Aboard ship, most pilot berthing was four to a room one level below the flight deck in spaces either forward or aft of the hangar deck. Upper and lower berths were permanently affixed, rather than being "fold down," and were on opposite sides of the small rooms. There was a desk and a safe for each pair of bunks, and there were four lockers. A light at the head of each bunk permitted one to read without bothering the others. A modicum of privacy in the room was provided by a curtain across the open hatch — the door. A steel rim ran about six inches high across the bottom of the hatch, which is standard across all exits and entrances in ships to minimize the sloshing of any water that might come aboard. It doesn't take too many barked shins before the novice at sea learns to step high.

CarDiv 22 departed San Diego for Hawaii in mid-January 1944 with Lieutenant Commander Harvey Feilbach as the air group commander as well as commander of VF 60. For flight operations, the basic unit of the fighter squadron in World War II was a two-plane element called a section. Two two-plane elements formed a division, and any number of divisions could fly together. Single-seat fighters have nothing firing aft, so the advantage of the element and division structure was mutual protection. As an example, if a two-plane element were under attack, the two planes would separate to a distance compatible with their radius of turn. Then when the enemy made a run toward one of the planes, both planes of the element would turn toward each other with the plane not under attack having a clear shot at the enemy. When they again turned to resume their original course, they would be in a position to repeat the maneuver but would have changed sides. This scissoring defense was known as the "Thach weave" (after John "Jimmy" Thach, a commander in the Navy who created the maneuver as a defense mechanism) and could be done equally well by the two elements of a division as by the two planes of an element. Because of this interdependence of a section leader and his wingman, it was standard doctrine that a wingman should never leave his leader. I was assigned to fly as wingman on the squadron commander. As with all unit commanders in the Navy, Feilbach was referred to as the "skipper" and his radio call was "Cap." I was "Smitty" and the others in the division were Royce "Lip" Singleton and Edgar "Eggbert" Barber.

The skipper scheduled a practice mission for the entire air group on 18 January 1944, and we bored a hole in the air for about two and a half hours. We performed a number of practice maneuvers, including a climb to 20,000 feet, which is an altitude that can lead to hypoxia in some people. After coming to know Feilbach better, I think it probable that this excursion into the upper air was done deliberately to teach pilots that they should carry their oxygen masks on all hops. Most of the pilots on that flight did not have their masks, though none appeared to suffer from oxygen deficiency.

I learned another lesson during the landing after that flight. For carrier operations, planes entered their landing pattern by flying parallel to the carrier's course to pass low and abeam the carrier on the starboard side. When adequately ahead of the carrier, the lead plane peeled off in a left-hand turn. Successive planes peeled off in intervals of about 20 seconds. Landing cockpit checklist was completed on the downwind leg; it differed from the checklist for a runway landing in requiring extension of the tail hook and the unlocking of the tail wheel.

When Cap's division dropped into the landing pattern that day in January and I moved the switch to extend my tail hook, no green light appeared to indicate that it was down and locked. The tail hook was one of the few things on the F6F that operated electrically rather than hydraulically, so I immediately checked the battery voltage. I got a zero reading, and with no electricity I couldn't use the radio to ask for advice. I remembered that there was a manual override to lower the hook; however, though I looked high and low behind and to the right side of the seat where I thought the handle was located, I couldn't find it. If I didn't get the hook down, I had the options of a barrier crash or a water landing; neither was attractive. Fortunately, I also remembered that if a weak battery is turned off, it will to some extent regenerate, so I turned off the battery and all electrical equipment. I stayed in the pattern, and as I came downwind, I re-energized the battery and placed the hook selector switch in the down position. There was a pause, and then the green light came on. I breathed easier and made an uneventful landing. I can guarantee that I was not on deck very long before I knew exactly where that manual override handle was and, in addition, how the pilot operated every other override system on the airplane. I am not sure that Confucius made the following observation, but if he did not it is worthy of him: "If one survives, he becomes wiser."

It didn't take too many days of flight operations at sea in an operating squadron to bring home the fact that carrier operations were much different than operations from a land base. As with any new undertaking, there were things that were not anticipated. At sea, it was (and still is) mandatory that the pilot obey immediately and exactly the signals of the taxi director when an airplane is moving on the deck under its own power. This requirement results from spatial limitations with safety or disaster differentiated by only inches. Spotting (parking) aircraft on a pitching and rolling flight deck where aircraft are parked within a few inches of each other is a far greater challenge than it is on land.

Landing the first plane of an airborne squadron on a World War II-type carrier's empty flight deck was part of a precise and complex procedure. After the plane had landed and had been brought to a stop by the arresting gear, the pilot allowed the plane to roll backward a few feet to relieve tension in the arresting cable. A crewman from the arresting gear detail disengaged the hook and a yellow-shirted taxi director signaled the pilot to retract the tail hook. With the hook still on its way up, the same crewman gave the signal to taxi forward. The pilot immediately applied almost full throttle — though for a very short period of time — to expeditiously move forward to clear the landing area for the next aircraft. Speed in clearing was critical because the next aircraft could be landing in not more than 20 seconds. The old axial deck carriers of World War II were configured so that the landing aircraft landed in the direction that the ship was moving, *i.e.*, parallel to the keel. The modern canted deck carriers have the landing area inclined a few degrees from the main longitudinal axis of the carrier, so that any plane missing the arresting gear can fly off again without hitting aircraft parked on the forward end of the flight deck.

The barriers, arranged in a series of three, consisted of a set of three or four vertically spaced cables that were elevated into a vertical plane athwart the ship by hydraulically operated steel arms. When erected, the height of these cables was such that they would tangle in the propeller of an impacting aircraft. The cables would be pulled free of the steel arms and the aircraft would be quickly stopped by hydraulic damping. When not in use, the barriers were folded down to be flush with the flight deck. With the postwar advent of jet aircraft, the steel cables in the barriers were replaced with nylon netting, because the absence of a propeller allowed the cables to slide over the nose of the jet and across the canopy into the cockpit, which could decapitate an unfortunate pilot.

When the aircraft was past the barriers, the taxi director signaled a stop and gave the sign to the pilot to fold the wings, which was done by disengaging the safety pins and moving the hydraulic selector to pull the locking pins, allowing the wings to swing free. Crewmen on both sides pushed inward on the wings to fold them back. Once in place, the wings were secured in the folded position. The taxi director then brought the plane forward to where it was to be parked.

The first plane to land was taxied to the port side of the flight deck with its left wheel running within a few inches of the edge of the deck. From the cockpit, the pilot's view to either side was limited by the folded wings, and all he could see on the port side between the wing and the fuselage was water far below him. As the plane neared the forward edge of the flight deck, the taxi director moved close along the starboard side of the fuselage just ahead of the wing. He continued to bring the plane forward until the wheels

Free-run launching of a flight of F4Fs illustrating the congestion on a flight deck. The planes behind the F4Fs are SBDs.

were within a foot or less of the edge with the engine and propeller extending well beyond the end of the flight deck. It was bad enough from the pilot's position with nothing visible in front of him or to the left but the ocean 70 feet below, but it must have been worse for the taxi director, who was positioned in a highly restricted space on the very edge of the flight deck. This operation was particularly nerve-racking in a heavy sea when the ship was pitching and rolling.

The next three planes were also spotted on the bow in essentially equally precarious positions. It must be obvious why instant obedience on the part of the pilot is mandatory. A second's inattention or a foot slipping off the brake and plane, pilot, and taxi director would be over the side. Those four forward spots made most pilots nervous.

Another uncomfortable aspect of the carrier flight deck was the smoke from the stack. World War II carriers were all fueled with oil that was burned in boilers to produce steam, which in turn ran the turbines that drove the screws — the propellers. Steam also powered the donkey engine — the small auxiliary engine — that moved the large rudder. Obviously, the exhaust from the boilers had to be vented. On the *Suwannee* there were two stacks, one on either side of the ship, the tops of which were on a level with the flight deck. Smoke could be vented through either stack, and it was up to the Officer of the Deck on the bridge to select the appropriate one. The appropriate stack was, of course, the lee stack to carry the smoke away from the ship. However, during zigzagging or during the turn into the wind to begin flight operations, it was not always possible to shift stacks quickly enough. From the pilots' point of view this was most serious during the turn into the wind for launching. In that case, the turn was executed when pilots were in their planes on the after portion of the flight deck with engines running. It frequently happened that, during the turn, the hot, high-sulfur, effluent gas from the stack would be blown across the flight deck. This was nasty stuff to breathe. Unfortunately, there was no choice.

After reaching the Hawaiian Islands, all of the ships that were to rendezvous there anchored in the roadstead between the islands of Molokai and Maui. We "rode the hook" — anchored — for about three days while the fleet assembled for the invasion of Kwajalein atoll in the Marshall group. We then set sail for Kwajalein without having set foot on shore.

It doesn't take long to become accustomed to the routine of carrier life. A ship is never quiet. Below decks the sound of ventilators is ever present, and on deck or in the catwalks there is water noise associated with the ship's passage. Noises from flight operations were the worst for pilots when in their sleeping quarters, especially if they were aft of the hangar deck. The impact of landing aircraft on the flight deck immediately overhead was a jarring experience. For those quartered forward, the firing of the catapult was as bad or possibly worse. The noise associated with raising or lowering an elevator also became quite familiar, as it came clearly into the sleeping quarters through an intervening one-eighth-inch-thick steel bulkhead. Fortunately, the elevators were rarely used at night — blackout conditions made hazardous any movement of aircraft. Night launchings by catapult were common, but night landings were relatively rare.

Early in the voyage, while still relatively distant from Japanese territory, fuel was conserved and wear on airplanes was minimized by limiting both the number of patrols and the number of planes per patrol. En route, the three carriers rotated responsibility for the duty. Each carrier was responsible for the combat air patrols (CAPs) and anti-submarine patrols (ASPs) every third day. However, the size and number of patrols increased as the fleet neared its destination. On 25 January 1944, the first glimpse of the Marshall Islands was obtained while on an otherwise uneventful CAP high over the ships. There was nothing particularly impressive about this atoll in terms of its size or other physical characteristics, and it was probably uninhabited, but it was Japanese and that was enough to stimulate wonder as to what would come next. Also on 25 January, the *Sangamon* had a bad deck fire due to an F6F breaking through two barriers to crash on the forward end of the flight deck; several people were killed. Later the same afternoon, after the fire was extinguished and the debris was being cleaned up, a TBM went through the third barrier, damaging four more airplanes.

In the afternoon of 26 January 1944, some additional excitement was provided by a mid-ocean collision. The *Suwannee* was the duty carrier, providing the CAPs and ASPs. For flight operations, the duty carrier had to leave formation and steam to the rear to launch or recover aircraft. A number of pilots were in the ready room reading and utilizing one of the few areas in the ship with even a semblance of air conditioning. Suddenly, over the squawk box the general alarm was sounded with a warning for personnel to stand by for a collision. After waiting, more waiting, and yet more waiting, nothing happened. Over ten minutes must have passed, and it seemed that there had been a false alarm. About that time, the impact occurred. It was not particularly violent, but the ship seemed to rear up, stop, and then slowly back astern.

The details of events leading to the collision were learned later. It seems that Admiral Ragsdale had given the "execute" order for the *Suwannee* to depart formation to conduct air operations. This order called for a reversal of course to port. The Admiral or his staff had not taken into consideration the coincidence of his order with the zigzag pattern of the fleet, which at that moment called for a 60-degree turn to starboard by all ships other than the *Suwannee*. As a result, the *Suwannee* was turning left while the *Sangamon* was turning right. They approached each other bows on. Though the momentum of two 12,000-ton behemoths defies rapid deceleration, the distance of separation was such that both ships could be slowed considerably before impact so that the result was not catastrophic. Captain W. D. Johnson ordered the starboard screw into full reverse and stopped the port screw. This both slowed the turn and slowed down the momentum of the ship. The *Sangamon* also put screws into full reverse.

Captain Johnson's actions avoided a full bow-to-bow meeting at hull level. Rather, the bows passed to the starboard sides of each other, carrying the *Suwannee's* port catwalk back to the forward port 40-mm gun sponson — a circular tub welded to the side of the ship — and compressing the forward 20 feet of flight deck. Though the *Suwannee* was by then moving at no more than a walk, the impact caused the bow of her flight deck to be bent upward by one or two feet; ever afterward, aircraft were thrown upward into the air as they cleared the flight deck on takeoff. The severity of the *Sangamon's* damage was somewhat less, and both carriers remained capable of supporting flight operations. Captain Johnson was ultimately blamed for the mishap, but nobody aboard the *Suwannee* believed it to be so. Certainly Admiral Ragsdale or his staff deserved at least partial blame. I was pleased to learn later that this blot did not affect Captain Johnson's career; during the postwar era, during a refueling stop at NAS Memphis, I found he was Admiral in command of the Air Station and Naval Air Technical Training Unit there.

Kwajalein

Both Kwajalein and Eniwetok in the Marshalls, like Tarawa in the Gilberts, are coral atolls, rings of small coral islets surrounding a central lagoon. An invasion of Kwajalein was scheduled for late January 1944. A preliminary "softening up" strike was made on Kwajalein by planes from the fast carrier forces on 4 December 1943. The efficacy of the Hellcat as a fighter was proven during this operation when 91 F6Fs tangled with 50 Mitsubishi A6M Zeros and destroyed 28 of them with a loss of only two F6Fs. On 31 January 1944, Air Group 60 and the air groups from other carriers began strikes on the larger fortified islands of the Kwajalein atoll.

VF 60 pilots and flight surgeon at the time of the Marshall invasions.

These strikes preceded troop landings on the 31st and continued in close support of the assault even after troops were ashore. CarDiv 22 was assigned as the Northern Carrier Air Group to support operations on Roi and Namur (code-named Burlesque and Camouflage) and with Air Group 60 did a lot

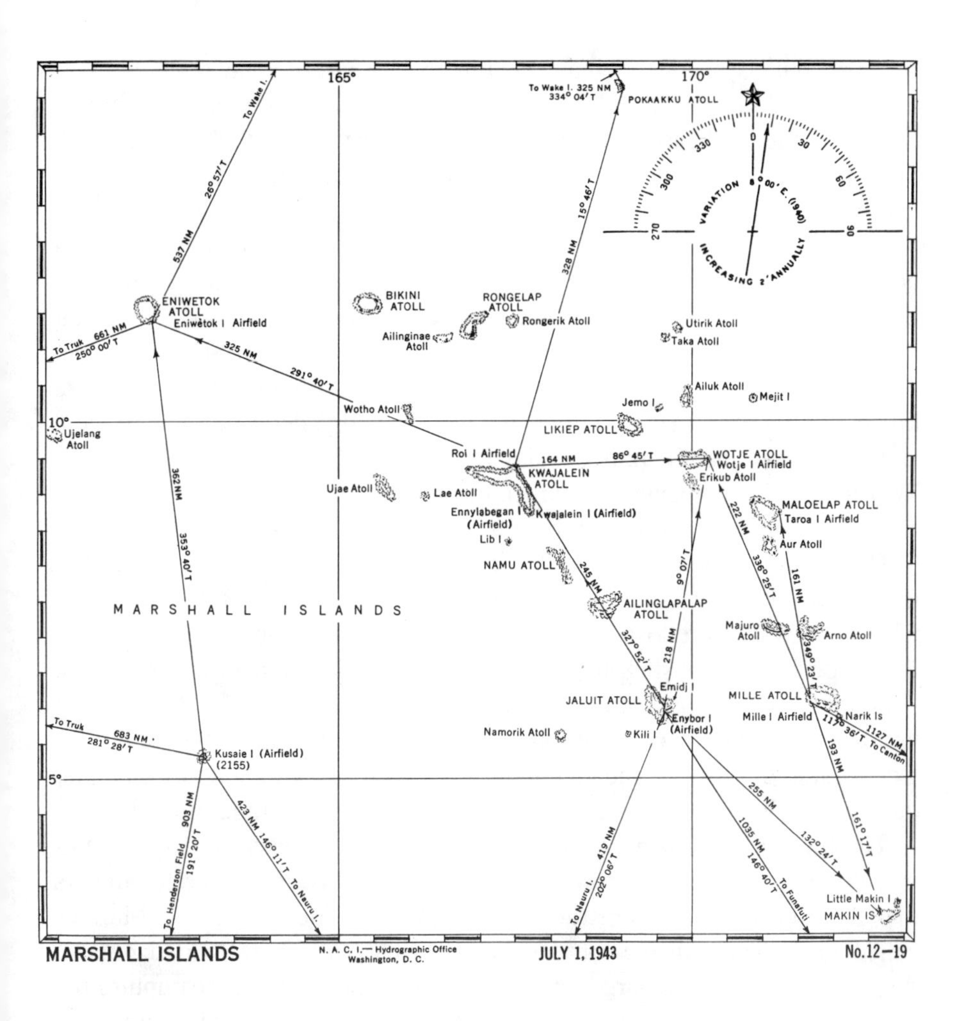

of bombing and strafing there. CarDiv 24 with the *Manila Bay, Coral Sea,* and *Corregidor* were the Southern Carrier Group to support operations at Kwajalein island in the south of the atoll.

There was a garrison of about 8,000 Japanese on the atoll, and they fought tenaciously. Some of the radio communications of U.S. tanks could be monitored, and in combat these were mostly in plain language rather than code. From their transmissions it was evident that the fighting, while not prolonged, was fierce. After the war, a former Navy Seabee (CB, construction battalion) recounted the efforts of the Seabees to make the airfield on the islet of Roi operational while the fighting was still in progress. To dodge

Japanese bullets, this gentleman spent the better part of a day and a night in the bucket of a scoop shovel. When the fighting was over, there were only a couple of hundred Japanese prisoners — the rest of the 8,000 were dead. Such fatal dedication to duty typified the Japanese soldier throughout the Pacific war.

During one strike on the first day of operations, two *Suwannee* SBD dive-bombers and an SBD from the *Chenango* collided while entering a dive on a target on the tiny islet of Ennumennett. Both *Suwannee* pilots, Lieutenant Byron Strong and Ensign Bill Sackrider, and the gunner in Strong's plane, Aviation Radioman Philip Barton, went down with their planes and were killed, as was the *Chenango* pilot. All were friendly, dedicated young men, and Strong had just the previous day logged his 1,000th hour of flight time. Two gunners did manage to parachute into the lagoon where small craft from the invasion fleet picked them up.

During other operations, two *Suwannee* torpedo bombers were forced to make water landings, and in both instances the radiomen, Bill Proctor and Charlie Oleson, were lost, apparently because the bomb-bay doors had collapsed on impact causing an inrush of water to pin the men to their seats. With their loss, it was recognized that water landings in the TBM torpedo bomber were extremely hazardous. To prevent additional losses, radiomen were required to ride in the greenhouse between the pilot and turret gunner during takeoffs and landings rather than at the normal station in the belly.

The feedback that came to the *Suwannee* from the beach was that bombing was effective against most targets but not against the concrete bunkers that the Japanese had constructed. This was rectified when the Marines called in strikes with the torpedo bombers carrying 2,000-pound bombs. Apparently, even these large bombs were not heavy enough to rupture the roofs of the bunkers, but the concussions from their explosions were sufficient to stun the people inside, allowing the Marines to do their job.

We replacement pilots, "new boys," didn't get to participate in much of the action during this, our first invasion. However, a few events are worthy of comment and illustrate the developmental process of a novice fleet aviator.

My logbook shows that I flew a large number of hours during the period of the Kwajalein invasion, but I was restricted to CAP duties. On one such flight, the skipper, Harvey Feilbach, and I were patrolling at 10,000 feet with broken clouds all around, both above and below. He started doing mild aerobatics that became progressively more stringent. We were in and out of the clouds, upside down, right-side up, in vertical banks, climbs, and dives.

From where I sat, it looked to me like he turned his ship "every way but loose." After about a half-hour of this he brought us up into a very steep wingover and came down, aimed at very thick cloud. I barely had time to cut inside on the turn to tuck in tightly before we penetrated the cloud. Within it we boiled along for a period of time with my wing stuck in his cockpit when, quite unexpectedly, he seemed to roll into a vertical bank and disappeared. His maneuver was much too quick for me to follow, and I had committed a wingman's one unforgivable sin — I had become separated from my section leader.

I got clear of the cloud and called to him on the VHF radio. He didn't answer. In my chastened state I flew around in a search pattern. It didn't take too long to spot him, so I rejoined with no further communication. In the ready room after the flight, nothing was said. That evening, after flight operations had ceased for the day, I came up onto the flight deck to get some fresh air. The skipper was standing near one of the planes examining it. I walked over and told him I was sorry to have lost him in the cloud and that I would try my best to see that it never happened again. In his characteristic taciturn manner, he turned slowly and looked at me. The only thing he said was, "You're a better pilot than I thought you were," and he walked away. I was dumbfounded. It hadn't dawned on me that he was testing me and was simply trying to see what he had to do to lose me.

Harvey Feilbach had consideration and feeling for his pilots and an interest in their safety and wanted to develop their performance to their maximum capability. Many pilots seemed unaware of the skipper's intent at the time and have only developed an appreciation with the maturity of passing years.

Kwajalein was also the first place that the squadron was on the receiving rather than contributing end of a bombing raid. After operating from 31 January through most of the first two weeks of February 1944, the carriers were running short of stores, so orders were received to proceed into Kwajalein lagoon for replenishment. Fighting on the islands was in the mop-up stage. Anchors were dropped and needed stores began to come aboard.

Replenishment required an overnight stay, and it wasn't too long after dark that the "general quarters" alarm was sounded. At that time, the general quarters station for all pilots was the ready room. When pilots arrived, they were informed that an air raid was in progress and were instructed to sit down and relax. The raiders were believed to be Japanese Mitsubishi G4M twin-engine bombers, code-named "Betty," from Eniwetok. All ships in the anchorage made smoke to obscure their positions. The raid lasted for two or

A Japanese Betty bomber. (Photo, U.S. Air Force)

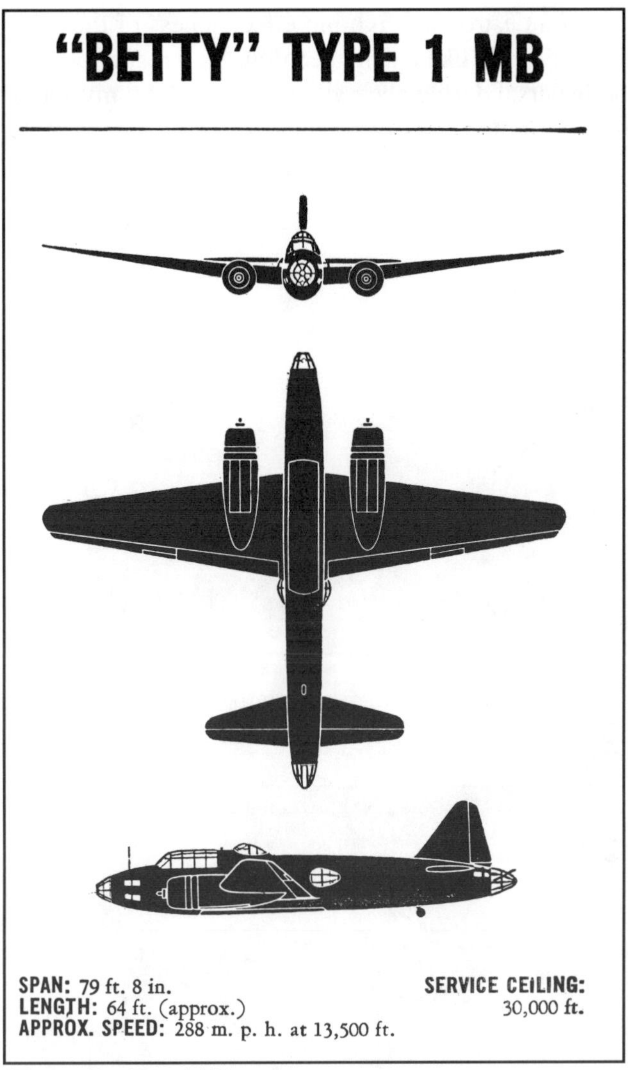

(*Recognition Pictorial Manual*)

three hours, boring to the pilots but an eternity to those on the beach; casualties there were very high. The "secure from general quarters" was finally sounded, and personnel were able to sleep during what was left of the night.

It appears, however, that someone in authority thought about this situation after the fact and realized that it was a very stupid thing to assemble all of the pilots in one location during such a raid; one hit in the vicinity of the ready room could destroy the fighting effectiveness of the ship. An aircraft carrier without pilots is like a defanged dog. As a result, other stations were assigned for dispersal during general quarters at night; my station turned out to be the after portion of the flight deck.

Chapter 4

Eniwetok and Beyond

THE invasion of Kwajalein had gone so well that the planners at JICPOA (Joint Intelligence Center, Pacific Operations Area) decided to advance the scheduled invasion of Eniwetok to 19 February 1944. Eniwetok, another atoll in the Marshall group, lies roughly 325 nautical miles (375 statute miles) west-northwest of Kwajalein. CarDiv 22 was released from duty at Kwajalein after flight operations on 12 February, and after the aforementioned anchorage in the Kwajalein lagoon, proceeded to Eniwetok.

The carriers arrived off Eniwetok and initiated strikes against the atoll on 16 February 1944. The skipper now considered the replacement pilots to be sufficiently experienced to fly strikes as well as combat air patrols and scouting missions. For the fighters, the strikes were strafing missions, primarily against the two islets of Eniwetok and Engebi, both of which had airstrips. This was not nearly as dangerous over an atoll with its limited land mass as it was later found to bc over broader expanses of solid terrain. At an atoll the strafing planes could make their approaches from over the ocean and depart across the lagoon over a non-populated region, or vice versa. Thus the only place from which return fire was likely was the target area, and the Japanese were intelligent enough to restrict their firing at approaching planes, because the origin of such fire would receive an intense concentration of return fire. Such concentration from several aircraft is not trivial, because the F6F carried six 50-caliber machine guns, each with 600 rounds of ammunition. Since each cartridge weighed about one pound, this amounted to 1.8 tons of ammunition per plane that could be fired.

In February, the fast carriers had struck the important Japanese base at Truk, and though the significance of this was not immediately known, it later proved to have made an important dent in the Japanese strength in the Pacific. Even so, letters from pilots in the fast carrier fleet indicated that our pilots in Air Group 60 were getting more strikes per pilot per month than they were.

I learned during my first strike why the standard doctrine called for putting the guns on "high safe" after each run. Use of high safe put the breech blocks in the full aft position with no cartridges in the firing chambers. During air-to-air gunnery it was rare to fire a burst of more than six to eight rounds per gun, but during strafing two or three such bursts were frequently possible. Thus the barrels got quite hot. I was initially reluctant to jettison six rounds (one from each gun) after each run by putting the guns on high safe. Instead, I used "low safe," which allows the breech blocks to seat with cartridges in the chambers but turns off the electrical firing circuit. After my second or third strafing run, the guns started "cooking off" — firing slowly and randomly because the heat in the barrels ignited the powder in the cartridges. Obviously, this could be dangerous to another plane if it happened to be in the line of fire. Fortunately the "cooking off" occurred when I was well to the side and aiming at nothing but blue sky. However, I got the message and ever after used nothing but high safe.

The operation at Eniwetok went so smoothly and without serious mishap that on 26 February, CarDiv 22 was released with orders to return to Pearl Harbor, Oahu, Hawaii. The two major islets of Eniwetok and Engebi with their airstrips were safely in the hands of the Marines.

During flight operations, it was not unusual for a pilot to see strange and beautiful sights in the skies. I first observed an "aviator's halo" during the passage of ships to Pearl Harbor. A rainbow is produced by the sun's rays being refracted by the water droplets in a cloud. When a plane is above the clouds, its position allows observation of the full circle rather than the partial arc that is commonly seen, and because of the proximity of the plane to the cloud, the diameter of the circular rainbow is considerably smaller than that of the arc seen from the ground. When the plane is in the right position between the sun and the cloud, the plane's shadow appears in the center of the rainbow — this is the "aviator's halo" and is an absolutely marvelous sight. It is a typical example of the rewards that beckon men into the air. No words adequately describe the beauty.

We arrived at Pearl Harbor early in March 1944. As the ships sailed up the channel to enter the docking area, the battleships *Arizona* and *Oklahoma* could still be seen on the bottom on the far side of the harbor where they had been sunk 7 December 1941. In postwar years, the *Arizona* was made into a national monument.

After reaching Pearl Harbor, several things happened that affected the air group's future. We learned that the command at Pearl Harbor was considering replacing the ships' F6Fs with FM2 Wildcats — the F4F Wildcat built by General Motors — whose smaller size would allow 13 of them to replace our 12 Hellcats. But Lieutenant Commander Feilbach convinced the "powers that be" that F6Fs could be used in a dive-bombing role as effectively as the SBD Dauntless. The nine nonfolding-wing SBDs then aboard the *Suwannee* could be replaced by ten folding-wing F6Fs. The requisite space was equivalent, and an F6F could actually carry a larger bomb load than the SBD. Operation of the F6F as a dive bomber was possible by using the landing gear as a dive brake. This was done by placing the wheel selector in the down position at high speed. The wheels would then extend only partially where their drag was sufficient to allow diving at angles of 60 to 70 degrees without picking up excessive speed. After completing a bombing mission, the F6F could resume functioning as a fighter.

Feilbach's alternative was accepted, and the air groups on all the *Sangamon*-class carriers were reorganized. The nine fixed-wing SBDs were replaced on each of the *Sangamons* with ten folding-wing F6Fs, and VC 60 became torpedo squadron 60 (VT 60), flying TBM Avengers. The SBD pilots were ordered stateside for reassignment, and additional fighter pilots were added to bring the strength of VF 60 to a total of 30 pilots. The replacement pools at Pearl Harbor were full, and Harvey Feilbach could have chosen senior experienced pilots, but instead he chose a number of fresh young ensigns who had not yet been in combat. Harvey wanted to train them his way with an emphasis on safety of operation.

Logbook dates indicate that the ships spent about two weeks in Pearl Harbor at this time with constructive effort devoted to replenishing supplies and equipment in preparation for extended sea duty. The carriers sailed from Pearl Harbor shortly after mid-March 1944. The addition of more pilots led

A Douglas SBD Dauntless. (Photo, McDonnell Douglas Corp.)

The Grumman F6F Hellcat. (Photo, Grumman Corp.)

to a reorganization of the divisional structure in the squadron. Cap's division was revamped, with the skipper acquiring a new wingman, and I was moved to wingman of the second section, flying wing on John "Simp" Simpson. Lip Singleton became a division leader, with Eggbert Barber leading his second section. The only change in the torpedo squadron was that Butch Vincent, the former skipper of the dive-bombing squadron, remained behind to skipper the torpedo squadron.

Once at sea, the pilots were given a briefing on the coming operation. CarDiv 22 was en route to Palau in the far Western Pacific. The operation was to be a feint, suggesting a landing operation to throw the Japanese command off balance. Every major warship that was operating in the Pacific theater, including Australian and British as well as American, was to rendezvous for the operation. The purpose was to make this feint as realistic as possible to simulate a major thrust toward the Japanese home islands. The role of our particular carrier division was to provide air cover for the assembled fleet while the fast carriers made the actual air strikes on the islands. This was the *Suwannee's* only operation as a unit of the fast carrier fleet, and the CVE pilots envied the fast carrier pilots the chance to make the quick hit-and-run strikes with the opportunity of running up their scores in aerial combat. However, the unglamorous chores associated with air cover were very necessary for the protection of the surface ships.

Certainly the assignment of the *Sangamon*-class carriers to the provision of air cover was sensible, because the flank speed of 18.5 knots of the *Sangamon* class was quite inadequate to maneuver with the 30-knot fast carriers. This speed differential provided opportunity for the fast carrier divisions to move rapidly with frequent intrusion into areas where engagements with airborne Japanese planes were probable. In contrast, the regular role of the CVEs in close-air support tied the ships to the general proximity of the landing area where a prime function of the air groups was interdiction. Standard practice was to keep as many Japanese planes out of the air as possible, and this was accomplished by bombing Japanese airstrips and strafing their aircraft on the ground. Thus, CVE pilots didn't have many opportunities to accumulate high scores of Japanese airplanes destroyed in aerial combat. Even so, CVE aircraft usually managed to down the limited number that were encountered in the air, and before returning to the States, VF 60 had on the average shot down more than one Japanese aircraft per fighter pilot in the squadron.

By the route that the *Suwannee* took, the Palau Islands lay roughly 5,500 statute miles from Pearl Harbor. At her speed of 18.5 knots, a maximum dis-

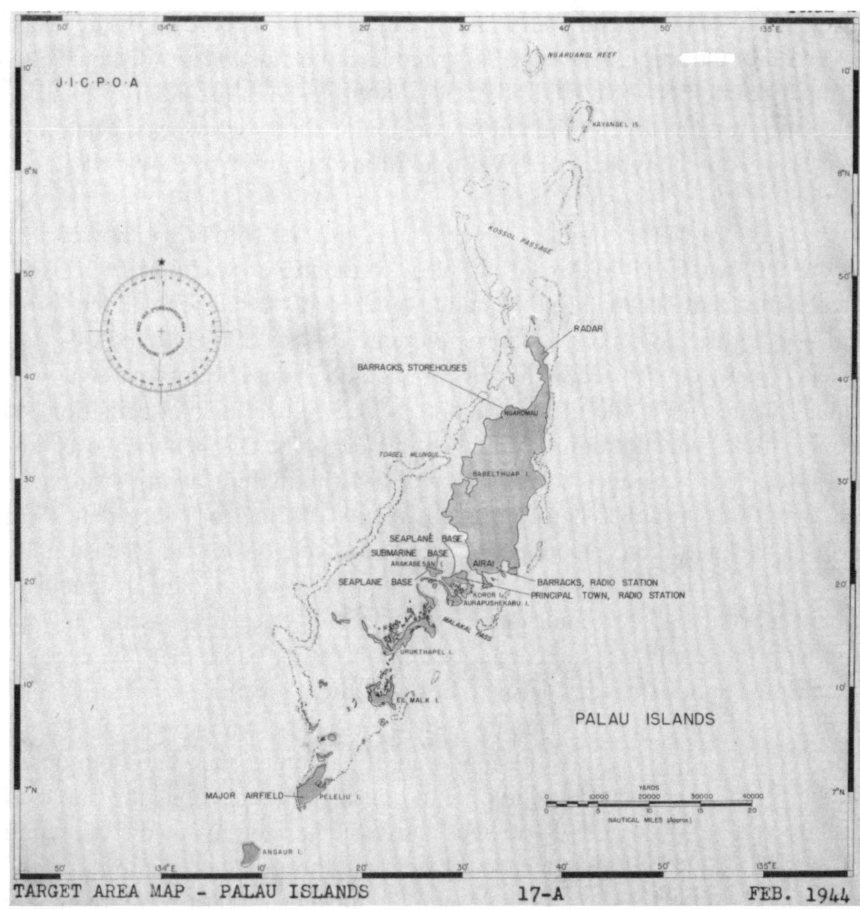

The Palau Islands.

tance of 444 nautical miles (or slightly over 510 statute miles) could be covered in a 24-hour period. However, this was further reduced by the zigzag patterns that were employed to frustrate enemy submarine attack. Zigzagging was standard procedure and involved frequent changes of course. Any given zigzag pattern involved cruising on a heading for a prescribed number of minutes followed by a port or starboard course change of a specified number of degrees. The time on leg, direction of turn, and the number of degrees were varied between one course change and the next. Over short periods of time the patterns were planned to appear random to a watching submarine commander, but over a time average, the patterns were designed to cover a mean course at a speed of 60 to 70 percent of the cruising speed of the ships. The zigzagging reduced the *Suwannee's* distance covered per day to between 300 and 350 statute miles and, for the trip to Palau, made the cruising time to the rendezvous point about two weeks. Such long cruises were not atypical of CVE operations during World War II in the Pacific.

Upon return to the States in December 1944, the ship's log showed that during the period while Air Group 60 was aboard, approximately 100,000 nautical miles of ocean (115,000 statute miles) had passed beneath the ship's hull — roughly equivalent to four circumnavigations of the globe. This represented many days at sea with many empty and listless hours between operations during which the officers and crew had to use their imaginations to provide their own entertainment and stimulation. The ship's library was limited in content, and an avid reader could finish anything worth reading in less than three months. Thus there was plenty of time for "acey deucy" (a form of backgammon), Monopoly, poker, and what have you. Occasionally the captain would allow one of the elevators to be lowered to the hangar deck so that a volleyball net could be stretched across the width of the elevator and the pilots could get some exercise. On the other hand, there were occasional interruptions to the routine that made life a bit more interesting. The course to Palau required crossing the equator. The course was chosen to make this crossing at the 180th meridian, the international date line, on 21 March 1944, the vernal equinox. Thus, during the crossing, the sun was directly vertical overhead, 90 degrees above the horizon in any direction one looked. The new "pollywogs" aboard were put through the "rite of passage" to become "shellbacks," and the special circumstances entitled all members of the crew to the titles "green dragons" and "purple porpoises."

It was shortly after this crossing of the equator that I made one of the worst carrier landings of my career. The experience was chastening because my landings were normally good, sufficiently so that other pilots had been complimentary. This was my first carrier landing after leaving Hawaii and occurred after we had made some practice bombing and strafing runs on a wooden sled that was towed 200 or 300 yards behind the carrier. Apparently I was somewhat rusty after our long layoff at Pearl Harbor.

What happened can best be described by comparing the actual event with a good carrier landing. The proper landing procedure called for the approaching plane to fly a flat, semicircular approach about 20 to 30 feet above the flight deck, which made it 90 to 100 feet above the water. The carrier steamed into the wind so that the wind line was straight down the flight

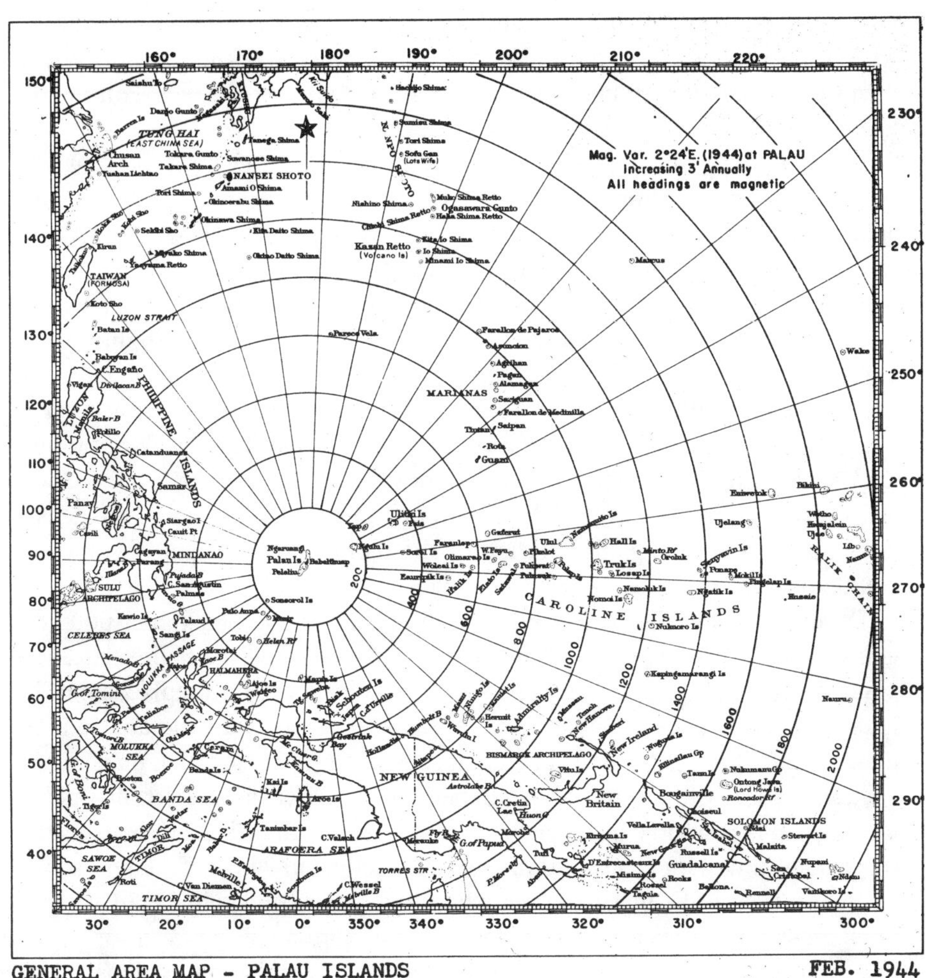

GENERAL AREA MAP - PALAU ISLANDS FEB. 1944

The Palau Islands in relation to other islands.

deck. Because of the relative motion of the approaching plane and carrier, entry from downwind flight into the semicircular turn was begun ahead of the carrier so that, as the carrier moved forward, the constant-radius turn was completed as the approaching plane arrived at the stern of the ship. Then if the height and speed of the plane were appropriate, the landing signal officer gave the "cut" signal to the pilot. Upon receipt of that signal the pilot took off all power and allowed the nose of the plane to fall slightly. He then came back rapidly on the stick to get the tail low to cushion the landing. If the timing was right, the tail hook engaged an arresting wire just as the three wheels were touching the deck. The hydraulic damping of the arresting wire then provided a smooth but rapid deceleration. Our average deck roll in an F6F after engaging a wire was approximately 44 feet.

My bad landing occurred because of poor timing. After I got the "cut," I allowed the nose to drop too far so that I couldn't bring the stick back fast enough to drop the tail wheel even with or below the main wheels. As a result, the wheels of the main landing gear hit first, making the plane bounce back into the air with nose high. The tail hook had, however, engaged a wire. Thus, while the plane was climbing ten or more feet above the flight deck, the arresting gear was killing its forward speed.

When the plane dropped back to the flight deck, it was very nearly a vertical drop. The result was that the plane was slammed hard back onto the deck — so hard that all three tires were blown and a number of rivets in the skin were popped. Because of the blown tires, I could not taxi and the deck crew had to push the plane forward of the barrier before flight operations could continue.

During the subsequent debriefing in the ready room, the skipper poured generously into my ear his dissatisfaction and expressed the belief that the plane would be out of service until we could off-load it for a replacement. I later checked with our maintenance chief to see if this was true and found that it was quite possible to effect repairs aboard ship. Indeed, that plane was back in the air within three days. (Experienced carrier pilots from that period may think it strange that I mention blowing three tires, because most carrier planes of the time had solid rubber tires on the tail wheel. Though I subsequently flew F6Fs that were equipped with such solid rubber tail wheel tires, those that we were using in mid-1944 were inflatable.)

CarDiv 22's course took it in close proximity to the group of Japanese-held islands known as Truk. Truk was to Japan a stronghold roughly analogous to what Hawaii was to the United States. In March 1944, Japanese strength in the Truk Islands was still considered to be formidable even though the fast carriers had made a damaging hit-and-run strike in February. Because our passage would be within 100 miles of this Japanese bastion, there was a serious possibility of detection of the carrier division by Japanese scout planes with ensuing attack by shore-based aircraft. As a result, the fighter squadrons flew a heavy schedule while CarDiv 22 was in the vicinity of Truk. All 44 fighters from two of the three carrier air groups were in the air throughout the passage. Patrol stations were at 10,000, 15,000, and 20,000 feet. The fighter squadron from the third carrier remained on ten-minute alert and was launched when it was necessary to land and re-fuel one of the airborne squadrons. Overall, the operation worked quite smoothly, and CarDiv 22's passage escaped detection by Japanese scouts.

In late March 1944, the fleet rendezvoused for the strike on Palau with the majority of Allied fighting ships from throughout the Pacific arena, including essentially all cruisers, battleships, and fleet carriers as well as many destroyers of American, British, and Australian nationality. In a period of a few hours, hundreds of ships arrived from all directions and effected an orderly condensation into a gigantic fleet. The morning after the rendezvous, aerial strikes were made on the Palau group beginning at dawn.

The USS *Santee* had joined the carrier division, and thus all of the *Sangamons* were in one unit. Because the four *Sangamon*-class carriers were the slowest among the carriers in the assembled group — indeed, probably the slowest ships in the entire fleet — we drew the short straw and were relegated to flying combat air patrol over and anti-submarine patrol around the assembled fleet. The fleet carriers made the actual strikes on the islands.

The first combat air patrol took off before dawn on the initial day of strikes at Palau. A group of *Suwannee* planes was assigned to patrol at 10,000 feet; patrol altitude was reached before daybreak. As the darkness began to dissipate, the size of the fleet became apparent. To say that the size was impressive is completely inadequate: it was awe-inspiring. The day turned clear, and from 10,000 feet we could see well over 50 miles.

But on that morning, ships extended across the surface of the ocean to the limits of vision. They were cruising in formation, rhythmically executing the same zigzag pattern. The firepower of that fleet was indescribable. It is doubtful that ever before have so many first-line fighting ships been assembled in the same place, and, indeed, probably never again. This fleet condensed and stayed together for two days of strikes and again evaporated to a diversity of destinations across that big ocean.

From the *Suwannee's* point of view, the only noteworthy incident during the Palau operation was the approach of a Japanese PT boat, which was sunk by the ship's gunnery crews before any torpedoes were launched. We four *Sangamons* departed to the south with the destination being Espiritu Santo in the New Hebrides.

Chapter 5

Aitape and Hollandia: A Relatively Easy Time

THE *Suwannee* continued south and arrived off the coast of Espiritu Santo in the New Hebrides on 7 April 1944. After nearing the island, the air group was scheduled to fly off the ship to land at an airstrip designated as Bomber 3.

Preflight briefing and manning of aircraft proceeded normally. In addition to his flight gear, each fighter pilot carried a flight bag with enough clothing and personal gear for a few days ashore. Prior to flight, this bag was stowed in the after portion of the fuselage through a small hinged door on its underside. After extended exposure to the tropical sun, the interior of the fuselage was invariably an oven, and as a result, this small area was known unlovingly as the "hell hole."

On this particular flight, after the bags had been stowed and the pilots had manned their planes, the air officer gave the command, "Prepare to start engines," on his bull horn. Engines were primed, and on the command, "Start engines," starter switches were hit. Most of the aircraft started immediately; however, one plane had smoke emanating from the lower right portion of the engine cowl and did not start. The pilot tried again, also with negative results. On this plane, the cartridge starter, then in general use on the F6F, had malfunctioned, and it was not going to work without extensive repair. The pilot, therefore, sat in the plane on the deck with a dead engine while the rest of the planes were launched.

He had resigned himself to sailing into the anchorage aboard ship and ignominiously going ashore by barge, but one of the yellow-shirted flight deck crew climbed up on his wing and told him that they were going to try a bungee start with a thick-stranded rubber cord. Though the pilot had seen bungee starts used on Curtiss SBC-4 Helldiver dive-bombers at the Naval Reserve Station at Fairfax Airport in Kansas City, Kansas, in 1939, he had never been directly involved; this attempt on the Hellcat was the one and only time that he saw it used during World War II.

The bungee cord was attached to a short, leather cuplike sleeve that was placed over the tip of one of the propeller blades. The blade was rotated into the horizontal position on the port side where it was on the upstroke. The bungee cord was run across the top of the propeller hub and was then stretched. This stretching can be done by a group of men, but on the carrier it was done by one of the tugs, the small heavy tractors used for moving aircraft about the deck. The pilot was then signaled to prime the engine, and one of the senior chief petty officers among the flight deck crew crawled under the airplane. He batted the down blade of the propeller until it had rotated far enough that the torque exerted by the stretched bungee caused the propeller to spin and start the engine. The purpose of the batting motion was to be sure that the chief's hand was moving fast enough to be clear of the following blade when the propeller spun. The combination of the tension on the bungee and the centrifugal force from the spin threw the leather sleeve clear on the starboard side of the airplane. The procedure worked quite successfully, and the single plane had the entire flight deck to itself.

The plane was taxied into position for takeoff and was launched. Because it had taken a bit of time for the full air group to rendezvous, they weren't too far ahead, and the lone plane soon caught up. The flight to the island was relatively uneventful, but a considerable fraction of the time was spent in the comparatively thick cloud build-up. The weather delay was compounded by a delay in clearance to Bomber 3, which had a single 5,000-foot runway cut out of the jungle at the edge of a coconut grove. It was paved with steel matting known as Marsden matting. Individual pieces of this matting were about ten inches wide by four or five feet long. Holes were spaced regularly to reduce weight and provide drainage. The pieces fit together with a tongue and groove array, reminding one of an overgrown erector set. But it worked quite well on a broad variety of surfaces, and the Seabees could lay an entire runway in a day or two.

Making an unarrested landing on such a runway after several months of carrier operation was quite a sensation. After touching down, the average pilot's reaction was that his plane was never going to stop rolling. At the end of the runway, each plane made for one of the dispersal areas, which were reached by taxiways that circled around, one on either side of the runway, from one end to the other. This airfield configuration was used extensively throughout the Pacific by both the Japanese and the Allies and was violated only when the topography restricted space. Even though land operations seemed strange after several months at sea, the air group must have done all right. That evening one of the local personnel was heard to comment to another that our group was certainly a sharp outfit; he noted that every plane made a three-point landing right at the end of the runway with consistent landing intervals of about 20 seconds.

Each dispersal area would hold several airplanes. Air Group 60 was spread through two or three of these areas, but all were in walking proximity so that operation as a unit was possible. From any dispersal area, one could walk directly into thick jungle. Of course all aircrew had to explore the jungle to practice the survival techniques that were then being taught. One particular technique for getting potable water was tried by most flight personnel. Each air crewman carried a hunting knife. In the jungle, this knife could be used to slice a section two or three feet in length from one of the numerous lianas (vines) that dangled down from the tree canopy. If the bottom and top slices through the liana were made on the bias and the length of liana was inverted, about a cup of water would drain forth. If the species of liana was such that the liquid was clear rather than milky, this water was potable. Furthermore, if another six inches or so were cut from the drained end, a second cup of water could be obtained, and this process could be repeated down to the last few inches of the cut vine. A Navy aircrew's interest in water is natural. One of the hazards of the job is the possibility of ditching at sea. If one survives to make it ashore, he is almost certain to be thirsty with a strong interest in quickly getting to a supply of water.

Berthing facilities on Espiritu Santo were Quonset huts that were screened at either end but otherwise open to the air. Bunks were ordinary canvas cots. It was normal to keep a few small lizards, probably geckos, in a hut to minimize the insect population; this actually worked very well. The huts were located in a coconut grove, and everyone had to try playing monkey to get at the coconuts. The pilots learned quickly that the ripe coconuts were very rich and that eating too much led to an excessive amount of time logged on the throne of a latrine. The same was not true of green coconuts. If the top was knocked off one of these, it provided a ready-made cup full of cool water tasting slightly tart with only a hint of coconut flavor. It took some practice to remove the husk to get at the hard, round, nutlike part found at the local grocery store in the States. Lianas, if available, were a source that could be tapped more quickly and easily.

Red Rynearson and I had an interesting evening with the Marine Corps while at Bomber 3 on Espiritu Santo. This occurred on the second or third night ashore when, during a walk in the relatively cool pre-dusk, we decided to examine a PBJ Mitchell, the Navy version of the Army North American B-25. A Marine squadron equipped with these planes had just arrived that afternoon, fresh from the States and eager to sally forth to win the war. Espiritu Santo had never been closer to the fighting than 500 miles, and by April 1944 it was relegated to a staging area far from the battle. However, these Marines were green. They had "Semper Fidelis" tattooed on their foreheads and wanted raw Jap meat for breakfast. Just as it was getting dark, we two stalwart Navy fighter pilots were naive enough to walk up a shallow incline to a dispersal area where the Marine planes were parked.

There was still enough light to make out dim outlines of the planes against the background of the jungle. When within approximately 50 yards of the first airplane, we were surprised to have the barrel of a 30-caliber carbine thrust at our stomachs. We were told in no uncertain terms to halt and identify ourselves; there was no choice but to comply. The Marine guard on the butt end of the carbine then called his sergeant, and repetition of identification was required. It turned out that these clowns had a guard on each individual airplane. In contrast, it took only a roving patrol in a jeep to monitor the combined total of all other aircraft on the field. This episode quelled interest in Marine aircraft of any variety, particularly the PBJ.

The *Suwannee* departed Espiritu Santo on 11 April, and once under way, the air group was informed that we were en route to the north shore of New Guinea with short stops scheduled for Tulagi in the Solomons and for Sea Adler Harbor in the Admiralties; the latter was to be the rendezvous with the invasion fleet. Tulagi, once the capital of the Solomons, was the first stop. After dropping anchor there, a number of natives in long, narrow, dugout canoes paddled out to the ship to trade fresh fruit and fish for whatever they could get that was useful to them. The length-to-width ratio of these shallow draft craft made their seaworthiness questionable, particularly so because they had no outrigger. Nonetheless, the natives were very much in control and appeared to be completely at ease with the existing water conditions. During a short visit ashore, the natives were found to be very well adjusted to their environment. Their ingenuity was evident in their use of bamboo for utilitarian purposes. Two items that they constructed stand out: a hut that was under construction and a system for providing a water supply.

A native village lay a short distance up a path that climbed rather steeply from the beach. This village was quite neat and clean and consisted of two rows of thatched huts that faced each other across a cleared area with 20 or so feet between the fronts and about seven in each row. The central hut on one side was the chapel that was supervised by Presbyterian missionaries. The walls and roofs of the huts were bamboo frames — bamboo poles lashed together with palm fronds and the frames filled with a thatching of palm fronds. Appropriate spaces were left unfilled to provide for windows and doors. The structures were quite airy and cool, and during a rain, they proved to be watertight.

A new hut was under construction near the edge of the village, and it was being built with speed and skill. About eight or ten men were at work with a supply of bamboo poles and palm fronds. The frame was, of course, started first with the bamboo being deftly tied together with tight, slip-free bonds. Before it was complete, some of the men were already adding thatch. This was done from the bottom up, just as shingles are put on roofs. In less than an hour, they had the structure almost half-finished.

On the far side of the village, the path continued into the jungle. Not far up this path was a small stream that had been diverted to carry water for drinking, washing, and irrigation. The pipes for the plumbing were long bamboo shoots of large diameter whose nodes had been drilled through to allow the passage of water. Admittedly, the system worked by gravity flow, but it got the job done. Western man may have available a much more diverse selection of materials, but innovative capability is by no means his alone.

I continued to explore up the path and I came to a rattan palm that had fallen across the way. A rattan is a nasty thing; its wood is extremely hard and it is covered with sharp, wicked spines. I gingerly made my way around it and walked on. I came to a sharp turn, and as I rounded the corner, I suddenly found myself facing a large monitor lizard. We both froze. He looked at me, I looked at him, and we both took off at top speed in the directions from which we had come. I cleared that rattan in one leap and did not slow down until I was back in the village. In retrospect, I think that lizard was

Orientation, Rendezvous Points and Anti-Submarine Chart
Training Exercises and Rehearsals — Cape Esperance Area
Task Group 53.1 and Task Group 53.2 — May 20 through May 25

Southern Solomon Islands showing Tulagi off Florida Island with Guadalcanal to the south.

only about four feet long, but I had only seen little fellows that were 8 to 12 inches long. When the surprise of the encounter is combined with the unusual size of the beast, it is not surprising that my adrenaline flowed. I explored no further and spent the rest of my time that day along the shore where I searched for interesting seashells and watched the hermit crabs scurry around in their adopted shell homes.

The landings in New Guinea were to be at Aitape and Hollandia, about

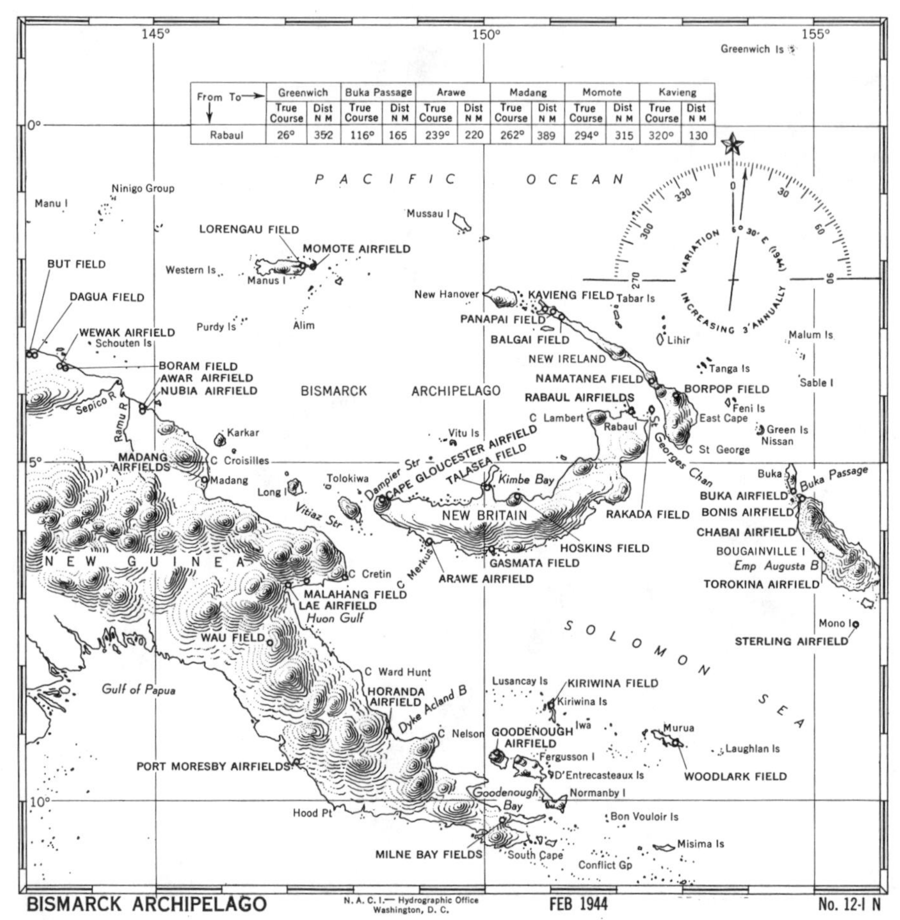

From ↓ To →	Greenwich		Buka Passage		Arawe		Madang		Momote		Kavieng	
	True Course	Dist N M	True Course	Dist N M	True Course	Dist N M	True Course	Dist N M	True Course	Dist N M	True Course	Dist N M
Rabaul	26°	352	116°	165	239°	220	262°	389	294°	315	320°	130

Eastern end of New Guinea. The Bismarck Archipelago and Manus in the Admiralties are prominent.

halfway across the northern coast of the island, and were to be made by Army troops. New Guinea is a big island, and the distance along the north coast from Milne Bay in the east to the Vogelskopf in the west is in excess of 1,000 miles. There is a high spine of mountains that runs down the middle of the land mass, so that the northern coast is effectively isolated from the southern. Aircrews were warned that, should they be forced down on the island, any interaction with native populations should be quite circumspect, since some of the tribes were still cannibalistic.

Enemy defenses at Aitape were softened up by a combination of offshore bombardment from cruisers and battlewagons and by aerial bombardment. VF 60 fighters got their first real workout as substitutes for the offloaded SBD bombers. However, as far as anyone could tell, the fighters were equally as effective in this bombing role. Antiaircraft fire was light and relatively ineffective. The air group suffered only slight damage to two TBMs, and it seems likely that in one of these cases the bomber had flown too low during a bomb drop and had been hit by its own bomb fragments. When the landings did occur there was very light resistance.

The softening-up process went on for two or three days before the actual landing of troops, which was on 22 April 1944. The pre-landing fireworks display outshone any Fourth of July celebration. In the first light of dawn, the bombardment from the heavy ships pummeled the shoreline defenses. During this period the first wave of troops were loaded into landing craft and headed toward their assigned landing sites. The cessation of the ship bombardment was the signal for the air controller to call in the aircraft strikes. In this case, the air controller was VF 60's own skipper, Harvey Feilbach, since he was the senior Air group commander in CarDiv 22.

In a sequence governed by the controller, bombing and strafing runs were made along the shoreline. After the aerial strikes, the first wave of landing craft were within a few hundred yards of shore, and those equipped with rocket launching racks let go a stream of 20 or more rockets in just a few seconds. It was spectacular. After this softening-up procedure, successive waves of troops hit the shore meeting very light resistance. Either there were not many Japanese troops or they lacked well-developed fortifications, possibly both. In any case, American casualties were few.

After Aitape, the ships proceeded farther west to Hollandia, also on the north shore of New Guinea. The situation there was already well in hand, though there were a few pockets of stiff resistance. Hollandia was more rugged with its own unique tropical beauty. Its main airstrip, on the landward side of a mountainous shore, was littered with wrecked Japanese aircraft as a result of multiple raids by the Army Air Forces.

VF 60 operations near Hollandia were, for wartime, rather peaceful compared to later operations in the Marianas and the Philippines. On one particular day, 12 fighters were assigned to fly combat air patrol over a destroyer that was acting as a picket doing radar and sonar surveillance. This destroyer was also the fighter-director station in control of the fighters. During long patrols with little to do but orbit on station, one gets tired of simply playing merry-go-round. It was not uncommon on such flights that, after a couple of hours, the monotony would be broken by doing some aerobatics, most often

Five TBFs in flight.

a "snake dance." This consists of getting all of the planes into a column and following whatever maneuver the lead plane initiates. Each plane chases the tail of the plane in front of him, and the result looks like a long snake writhing its way across the sky. On the day in question, the patrol was orbiting over the picket destroyer when the flight leader chose to initiate a tail chase. He swished his tail for the planes to trail into column. The flight had been cavorting for 10 or 15 minutes when the fighter-director station came on the radio: "Emerald leader, this is Freddie. You're looking good up there. Keep it up!" Apparently the monotony had been broken not only for the flight but also for the crew below.

When the Hollandia airstrip was made operational and Army P-47 Thunderbolts and C-47 Dakotas began to arrive in large numbers, CarDiv 22 was relieved and allowed to proceed back to the Admiralties. There some of the squadron managed to get ashore on the two biggest islands, Manus and Los Negros. A welcome supply of mail arrived on this visit to the islands. If you ask any man who has ever been in one of the military services, he will tell you that the receipt of mail is one of the bright moments of existence. Normally, mail came aboard only after it had arrived at one of the islands, so mail call was not a common event. The inverse was also true; letters could be put into the postal system only when in port. On rare occasions, mail might be brought aboard during a rendezvous at sea with a ship fresh from port. After we returned to the States, relatives commented that from the combination of reports in the newspapers and the arrival of letters home, they could follow reasonably well the peregrinations of the *Suwannee* around the Pacific.

The four *Sangamons* left the Admiralties and departed to the south with the destination again being Espiritu Santo, arriving in the vicinity on 13 May 1944. The air group was again scheduled to fly ashore, but the launch was to be a demonstration of catapult operations for a group of Marine pilots who were scheduled for catapult launch from a small carrier that would be ferrying aircraft. This small carrier was to have both a fully loaded flight deck and a fully loaded hangar deck, so there was no option but to launch by catapult. While aircrews were being briefed for the flight, a launch came alongside and the Marines came aboard. When planes were manned, the Marines were already on the flight deck in a group clustered around the base of the island.

When the ship turned into the wind, the launch was commenced. Each plane was brought forward, its wings were spread and the flaps lowered, and it was taxied into position and hooked onto the catapult. The catapult officer made a rotating motion with his signal flag, and the pilot gave the plane full throttle. If the instruments and feel indicated that everything was operating properly, the pilot indicated that he was ready to go by giving the catapult officer a salute. The catapult officer then checked the pitching motion of the ship and, as the bow started to rise, made a dramatic stretch forward pointing his arm, flag, and body in the direction of the bow. With this signal, the crew in the catwalk fired the catapult, and the plane was accelerated to more than 100 knots in the 90-foot length of the catapult track. The whole process was repeated every 90 seconds with the interval being determined by the time necessary to recharge the compressed air that drove the catapult. In comparison, when gross weights were light enough to free-run (without a catapult) down the flight deck, launch intervals were in the order of every 12 seconds.

The operation proceeded routinely. The air group rendezvoused and headed for the beach. This time the destination was Bomber 1, a strip near the coast by Pallikulo Bay on the southeast side of Espiritu Santo.

Chapter 6

Respite Before the Brouhaha in the Marianas

BOMBER 1 on Espiritu Santo was at a slightly lower elevation than Bomber 3, and because of land contours, the perimeter taxiways were less regular than those at Bomber 3. Otherwise, the general layout of one was much the same as the other. But because of the lower elevation and the humidity due to the close proximity to the bay, it seemed hotter than it had been at Bomber 3.

The squadron organization was again revised with me moving to become Lip Singleton's wingman. Because we had flown together in Cap Feilbach's division, we readily adapted to this new structure. Indeed, it was not long until we accidentally stumbled onto a maneuver that became our trademark — a somewhat different roll in formation for a flight of two. The unusual roll was developed as a result of being bored after a long, dull flight. The section was returning to the carrier when Lip decided to do a slow roll. He looked back at me and mistakenly got the idea that he had conveyed his intentions. He started the roll with what looked like a normal turn, so I banked with him and climbed as the degree of bank increased. The rotation continued until we were upside down with me above and slightly behind the leader. Continuation of the roll moved me down and to the far side. Upon completion of the roll, the two planes were in mirror positions of their original configuration.

These days with jets or small aerobatic airplanes with large engines, it is not unusual at air shows to see a whole formation rolling as a unit. What this requires is high horsepower-to-weight ratios. But with conventional World War II fighters, this was not common, though it may well have been possible if sufficient initial speed had been attained in a dive prior to initiating the maneuver.

The stay at Bomber 1 was for only three days, but on the 15th of May, after a day of idleness, I was looking for something to do and went over to the CASU (pronounced "cashew" and signifying Carrier Air Service Unit) on the south side of the strip. These units carried spare parts and overhauled aircraft. The spare parts could be checked out by carrier squadrons to replace those consumed during normal operations, and overhauled aircraft were given to the squadrons to replace losses or to trade for "war wearies" that needed some work.

I went into the CASU office that day to see if they had an F4U Corsair that I might fly. I made it clear that I had not yet flown a Corsair and that I would need time to study the handbook, a cockpit checkout, and a discussion with someone who had recently flown the airplane. I was informed that such an aircraft was available and that all the rest was possible, but there was another pilot ahead of me to fly the plane. Because I had nothing better to do, I decided to wait my turn and checked out an operating handbook for the F4U. While I was studying the book to learn the normal and emergency procedures for flying the plane, three crewmen from a shore-based patrol squadron came into the office. Apparently, their squadron flew Lockheed PV Venturas, but because of factors beyond their control, they would wind up at the end of the month deficient in flight hours. They would lose some of their flight pay unless they could log the requisite hours.

Their need was approximately three additional hours of flight time. The duty officer explained to them that there was an available Grumman TBM torpedo bomber that could carry all of them, but he had no one to fly it. Upon hearing this they turned to me and asked if I would take them up. I explained that I had never flown a TBM; however, I saw the TBM as a bigger, slower version of the Hellcat and felt that with relatively little time on the handbook, plus someone to show me how to start the thing, I would be comfortable in taking the machine into the air. If, under those circumstances, they wanted to make the flight, I would be glad to take them. They agreed without hesitation.

I then checked out a TBM handbook and took a few minutes to go through the major aspects of flying the airplane with particular note to engine operation, tab settings, system checks, emergency operation of all systems, and speeds for takeoff, landing, and stall. We proceeded to the dispersal area where the plane was parked and climbed aboard. I use the word "climb" advisedly because the pilot in a TBM sits in a cockpit about 13 feet above the ground. The plane captain, who was the ground crewman responsible for the airworthy status of the plane, stood on the wing and showed me how to start the engine; it fired with no trouble whatever. I did the initial cockpit checks and verified intercockpit communication with the three men riding in the back. While I was doing this, the plane captain had climbed down, and I gave him a thumbs-up indicating that I was ready to go. He had his assistant remove the chocks and gave me the signal to taxi forward, stopping me after I had cleared the other parked aircraft. This was followed by a spreading of his arms to indicate that I should spread the wings. I moved the hydraulic selector to do so and, when they were extended, locked them in place. From my vantage point in the cockpit, those 54-foot wings seemed to stretch into infinity. This was the biggest airplane that I had yet flown. (In retrospect, after having flown multi-engine aircraft with twice that wingspan, the wingspan of the TBM really wasn't all that much.) The plane captain signaled me that all was well, so I called the control tower for taxi clearance to the active runway and proceeded to the takeoff position. With run-up and checklist completed, takeoff clearance led to a normal and uneventful departure.

While I was getting the feel of the airplane, my passengers fired up the radar set, which was new to me since none of our fighters was equipped with such a device. They gave me bearings and distances to landmarks that they could distinguish on the radar scope, and we navigated to a variety of places throughout the archipelago. I found this novelty quite enjoyable.

After we had flown long enough to satisfy all of my passengers, we returned to Bomber 1. Considering that the TBM was a totally unfamiliar aircraft, I made a normal approach followed by a reasonably good landing, confirmed later by my passengers' positive comments. I signed their flight chits, and they departed in good spirits.

I returned to the CASU office to sign the flight sheet for the TBM to indicate its continuing airworthy status. The duty officer saw me and informed me that my proposed flight in the F4U was canceled. I asked why, because

I was looking forward to comparing the performances of the F4U with that of the F6F. He smiled and told me that I was lucky. The pilot ahead of me had gone off on a routine flight. A second pilot had appeared, and since I was not back, he had been given the airplane. He had no more than taken off when the engine torched and he went down in the jungle; a rescue team was trying to get him as we were speaking. To this day I don't know what happened to that pilot, because Air Group 60 departed early the next day. If the story has a moral, it is that it behooves one to do a favor for another human being, particularly when it doesn't cost you anything. You never know in what strange way you might be rewarded.

Departure the next day, 16 May 1944, took the air groups from Bomber 1 on Espiritu Santo to Henderson Field on Guadalcanal. Our planes taxied out of the dispersal area in sequence and proceeded to the end of the runway. Traffic was controlled from a tower that was a stilt-like structure atop four coconut logs; it was placed beside the runway midway along the length. The squadron was cleared as a group, then the skipper took off first with the rest of the squadron following at regular intervals.

This turned out to be a long, dull flight, and, even though the distance was only somewhere between 500 and 600 nautical miles over open water, it took more than four and a half hours. This was because over an hour had been wasted in getting all air groups rendezvoused, and then the fighters had to fly with a speed penalty because of the slow cruising speed of the TBM torpedo bombers. The carriers remained behind and the air groups were scheduled to meet up with them at a later date. Ground crewmen that were required for flight operations on Guadalcanal made the trip north aboard the torpedo bombers.

When Lip took the runway that day, he went to the left, or far, side. For me, his wingman, that takeoff was memorable. I assumed that he wanted to make a formation takeoff to save "join-up" time, so I taxied into position on the right, or tower, side of the runway. Though we rolled down the runway together and broke ground together, it soon became obvious that Lip was unaware of my presence, because almost immediately, with his landing gear in the process of retraction, he started a climbing turn to the right to buzz the tower. I was in a box with tall trees blocking movement to the right. The only possibility for preventing the distribution of random airplane parts along our direction of movement was to cross underneath him. I kept down, hoping that the top of my propeller would clear his belly, and as I passed underneath, my propeller tip was within inches of him. I was so low I expected my blades to grind into the runway surface. However, I believed that it was better to belly into the ground and slide down the runway with a reasonable chance to walk away from the accident than to slice my buddy's plane in two, leaving him no chance. Fortunately, Lip's wheels had by then completely retracted. The minimum clearance needed for me to safely pass under him would be just in excess of the diameter of the propeller, or in the order of 12 feet. He must have gained at least that much altitude by the time I crossed under, because I did get to the other side with no damage to either plane — though I still don't quite know how. Pulling a dunderhead stunt like that made me feel like an ass, but it had one benefit — survival is sweet and I appreciated being alive.

Air Group 60 was on Guadalcanal from 16 May until 23 May 1944. Guadalcanal was the first island that the Allies took back from the Japanese with landings by the Marines in August 1942 and with fighting on the island continuing into February 1943. It is at the southern end of the Solomons and lies to the south across Sealark Channel from Tulagi. Only San Cristobal lies farther south. After the fighting in 1942, Sealark Channel was commonly known in the U.S. Navy as "Iron Bottom" Sound because of the large number of U.S. and Japanese ships that were sunk there, the most numerous occurring during the night engagement that has come to be known as the Battle off Savo Island. This battle was between surface ships — cruisers and destroyers — without the participation of air power. In 1944 the sunken hulls were quite visible through the clear water when the sea surface was relatively calm; presumably, this is still the case.

Guadalcanal was a hot, humid, thoroughly miserable place. Living quarters were Quonset huts that were located where no breeze blew. Heavily chlorinated drinking water was supplied in large canvas bags — Lister bags — that were hung outside the doors of the huts. Outdoor showers were available but were fed with salt water that was pumped from the ocean so that after a shower, when you dried, you were grimy with salt residue and felt just as dirty and uncomfortable as before. These palatial quarters were disaffectionately referred to as the "Hotel de Gink." The air groups' mission on Guadalcanal was to practice for a landing invasion on unspecified islands of larger land mass than the atolls with which the pilots had become familiar. Cape Esperance on the northwestern end of Guadalcanal served as the area for the invasion practice. Flight operations were off Henderson Field, which was paved with Marsden matting at that time.

Lip and I by this time had flown together sufficiently that our two planes functioned almost as a single unit. The "snarl up" at Bomber 1 before coming to Guadalcanal had been an anomaly. During one of the practice strikes that were flown out of Henderson, we took off in close formation. An observer could see the wheels of our planes retract synchronously, intercooler doors close synchronously, and cowl flaps close synchronously. Later, over the target during the bombing run, both bombs fell away from our planes at the same instant. However, there was one thing during that flight that was not done together. On the way back to Henderson, Lip lost oil pressure. He called a "Mayday" (emergency) on the radio. I remained by his side to mark his position in case he had to land in the jungle and called Henderson warning them to keep other traffic clear so that Lip could land immediately if he managed to get back.

Lip handled the situation calmly and properly. He maintained a high power setting to overcome the friction of improper lubrication and plenty of altitude to optimize his choice of emergency landing sites should one be necessary. Fortunately, the engine kept running long enough for him to make the field and complete his landing, but the engine froze during the roll-out after the throttle was retarded. The plane stopped on the runway and had to be towed off. That type of experience makes pilots age more quickly.

Later at Henderson, during another emergency, an SBD Dauntless was observed making a low pass across the field in front of the control tower. It was obvious that the plane was in trouble; the right wheel of its landing gear was extended but the left gear was not. The tower must have told the pilot, because he climbed back into the pattern and cycled the gear. Again he made a low pass in front of the tower and again only his right gear was extended. After three repetitions of this sequence, it must have become obvious to the pilot that the left gear was stuck in the up position and was not going to extend. He then entered a landing approach with only the right gear extended. As he neared the runway, he kept a little power on the engine so that he would land with the tail wheel off the ground. He flew the plane to produce a gentle contact between the right wheel and the Marsden matting. Indeed, the contact was so gentle it was almost a kiss. As the plane slowed while rolling on that single wheel, the pilot maintained lift on the left wing by a combination of adding successively greater amounts of right aileron while slowly dropping the tail to increase the angle of attack. By the time the tail wheel touched the ground and full aileron was applied, the plane had slowed almost to the speed of a sprinter in a 100-yard dash. The left wing slowly dropped until the wingtip dragged on the ground, causing the plane to do a slow 90-degree turn to the left. With the left wingtip, the right wheel, and the tail wheel supporting the ship, the propeller had adequate clearance to rotate without damage, so the only repairs that had to be made were to the wingtip and to the left landing gear. The pilot had done an admirable job. His performance and that of Lip illustrate the skill and cool competence most often characteristic of the World War II Naval Aviator in the South Pacific.

While on Guadalcanal, a different type of experience happened to Dew Timm and me. On an afternoon that we weren't scheduled to fly, we decided to go fishing. We "borrowed" a three-man rubber life raft from a TBM, which we carried to the beach and inflated. Fishing gear was part of the emergency equipment in the raft.

Guadalcanal has a gently sloping beach, so launching was easy. However, it might be relevant to note that Guadalcanal has no good harbor, and the slope of the beach persists until well off shore. As a result, ships that supplied Guadalcanal were forced to anchor about a mile out and offload onto "lighters" — barges used for loading and unloading ships — that carried the supplies to shore. We had absolutely no luck near the shore, so we proceeded out beyond several offloading ships, almost into Sealark Channel.

All of the fishing lines were deployed and the raft was lazily drifting along under the push of a light breeze when one of the oars accidentally got knocked overboard. Because of the light weight and relatively high freeboard of the raft, the oar did not drift nearly as fast as the rubber raft and was thus being left behind. I jumped in and when the oar was retrieved started swimming back to the drifting raft. My swim was lengthened, but there was no reason to worry. No reason, that is, until I got close to the raft. At that point I got tangled up in the trailing fishing lines. These were meant to catch large ocean fish and were not easily broken. I didn't panic but found myself tiring rapidly in the tangled mess. I knew I was in trouble. Fortunately, Dew dog-paddled with his hands in the water to stop the drift of the raft. I was able to make the remaining few feet and climb aboard.

We headed for home, and though the distance back to the beach was only about a mile at the start, the wind blowing against us had moved the raft several miles down the beach and away from our base. Thus, we landed down the beach, a goodly distance from the "Hotel de Gink." We ended our fishing expedition sans fish and with a bulky rubber raft to drag home. It was dark when a couple of very tired and wiser lads climbed into their cots.

On 23 May 1944, we departed from Guadalcanal late in the day. The air groups flew out to rendezvous with the ships. When back aboard the *Suwannee* and settled into normal routine, I happened to glance at a calendar and realized that it was a couple of weeks past my birthday. I had passed the magic age of 21, which at that time was the age of majority, and had become a man with all rights and responsibilities of citizenship without even realizing it. Not surprisingly, I did not feel one whit different — there were other things to think about.

Air Group 60's role in the war was about to become more active. An initial briefing was given concerning the coming operation: we were to invade the Mariana Islands, and the first was to be Saipan. The Marianas had been chosen by the strategists because they were large enough to provide sites for airfields that would bring the Japanese home islands within range of the new B-29 Superfortress bomber, a plane we Navy pilots were unaware of at the time.

It was a good thing that one cannot read the future, because the action the *Suwannee* had seen to date would seem very mild compared to that which would occur during the next five months. At the end of that time, the ship would be put out of action from the visits by the kamikaze corps. During those five coming months, however, good old *Suwannee* justified her existence and gave more than she ever got.

Chapter 7

The War Gets Warmer: Saipan and Tinian

CARDIV 22 proceeded north from Guadalcanal to Kwajalein, which by then had become a peaceful backwater of the war. There, CarDiv 22 joined a fleet that was to participate in the Marianas operations. The Mariana Islands are volcanic in origin and are strung out generally north to south. Guam is the largest and southernmost island, roughly 30 miles long by 7 or 8 miles wide. Saipan and Tinian are the second and third largest islands; each is about half as big as Guam with lengths near 15 miles and widths near 5 miles. They lie slightly over 100 miles north of Guam with the smaller islands of Rota and Aguijan between Guam and Tinian. Other small islands form an irregular chain extending an additional 300 miles north of Saipan. To the east of the Marianas lies the Mariana Trench with ocean depths exceeding 5,000 fathoms (30,000 feet) over a considerable length and in one small region exceeding 6,000 fathoms (36,000 feet). There Mount Everest would disappear below the waves.

Army and Marine landings were to be made on Saipan, Tinian, and Guam with the initial landing planned for 15 June 1944 on Saipan. Preparatory strikes on Saipan began in advance of the 15 June landing. Air Group 60 was deeply involved from the time of its arrival at Saipan on 14 June. This was a period of intense flying. During the latter part of June into the first few days of August, pilots were pushed hard. For slightly in excess of six weeks we were in the air almost every day with the exception of a short respite when a quick run back to Eniwetok was made to replenish supplies, ordnance, and gasoline. This occurred during the shift in operations from Saipan and Tinian to Guam. An average flight took about four hours, but flights longer than five hours were not uncommon, nor was a schedule of two flights in one day. Pilots were less than comfortable strapped into their parachute and survival gear, all of which had to fit in a metal bucket seat. It did not take long to find out that the tins of water that were part of one's survival gear had sharp edges. The heavy flight load was further compounded by regular standing-alert duty (ready to launch in ten minutes) and by lack of rest due to night intrusions by Japanese aircraft. The fatigue associated with this regimen combined with the heavy Japanese firepower on the islands undoubtedly accounts for the number of the carrier's planes that were damaged during this operation.

There were three Japanese airstrips on Saipan and two on Tinian. Initial U.S. strikes were made to be certain that any remaining Japanese aircraft on these fields were rendered inoperable, and bombing efforts were intended to disrupt utilization of the runways and thus make it difficult for the Japanese to bring in aircraft from Iwo Jima or other islands to the north. The idea was to gain and control the air with superiority sufficient that troops on the ground would have nothing to worry them from above.

There was so much activity during this period that, with the exception of dates that can be verified from logs or publications, the order in which the following anecdotes are recounted has no real chronological significance. I simply relate the things that I can remember or that I have dug from records or the memories of others. These incidents are intended to be representative rather than exhaustive. This is not meant to denigrate or belittle the contributions and efforts of others, because pilots from many of the carriers could undoubtedly recount comparable experiences.

Including the four *Sangamon*-class carriers, there were 12 CVEs doing support work in the Marianas plus 4 more ferrying aircraft and providing air cover over oil tanker groups. On 17 June, two days after the troop landings on Saipan, five PBM Mariners arrived to provide long-range air search capability. They operated from a seaplane tender in Tanapag Harbor on the west side of Saipan. Saipan's Aslito airstrip was captured on 18 June, and as will

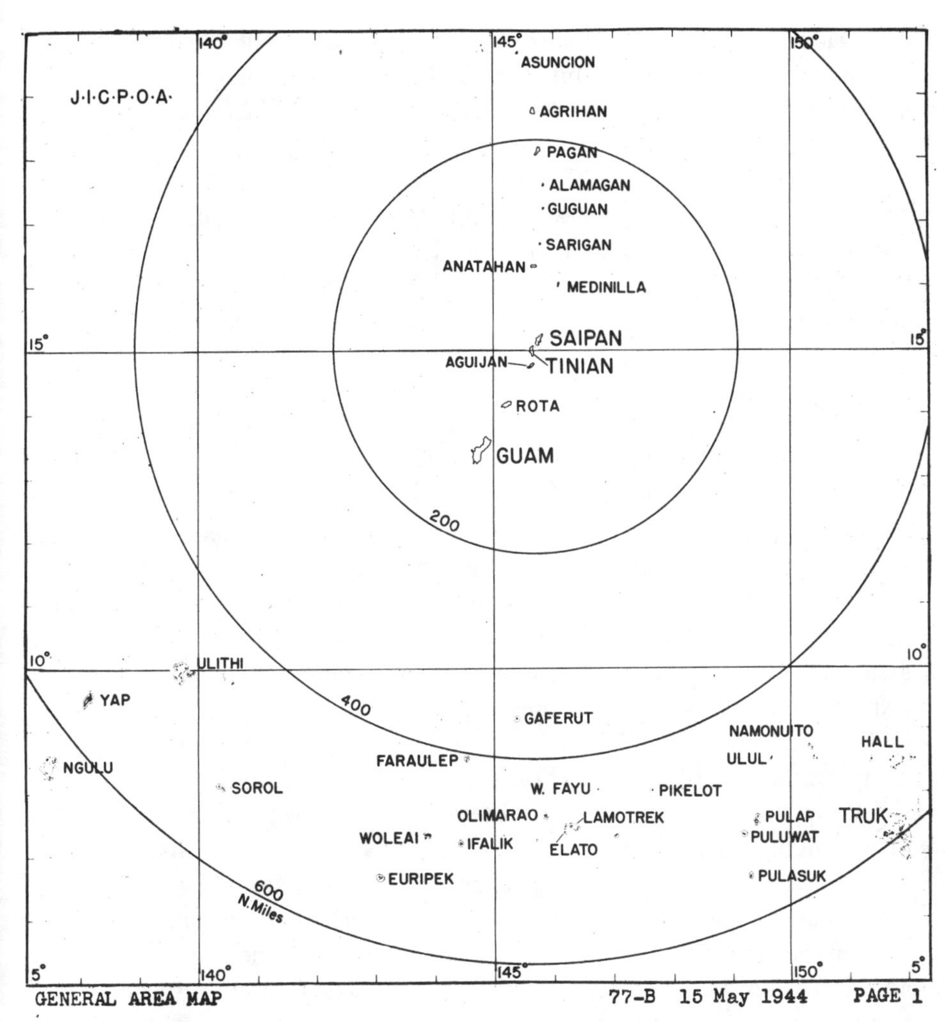

The Mariana Islands with the Carolines lying to the south. Distances can be estimated by noting that 1 degree of latitude equals 60 nautical miles.

become obvious from the experiences that follow, it almost immediately became an emergency haven. The Seabees had the strip operational in only a few days, and in approximately two weeks Army Air Forces P-47s were flown in and helped to supply both patrols and strike support.

Japanese antiaircraft fire, particularly over Tinian, was heavy and accurate. Many planes were hit during this period of operations, but only one pilot was lost: Lieutenant (jg) John Simpson, who was hit during a strafing run. Dacus and Kitzman quote Roy "Tex" Garner as placing this on 25 June and indicate that, after being hit, Simp headed for Saipan and the emergency strip at Aslito (64). However, he found that he could not make it and lost control of his aircraft during an attempted bailout. The plane went into a spin and hit the water. His body was later found with his chute unopened and his life vest uninflated. This contrasts with Frog La Fargue's recollection of the same event. Frog has stated that he was in the same flight as Simp and saw him enter a strafing run from which he went straight in without making any attempt to recover. It is not surprising that memories are imperfect after the intervening years. All that is certain is that Simp was lost during a strafing operation on Tinian.

None of the other *Suwannee* planes that were hit over Saipan or Tinian was actually brought down, though at least one was scrapped. In an early incident, Rabbi Shea received damage in the after section of his plane in the tail group. Red Rynearson was flying wing on Rabbi at this time, and he related that neither he nor Rabbi was sure that the tail would withstand a carrier landing. Because Aslito field (later renamed Iseley) in southern Saipan had been captured the day before, 18 June, by the Marines, it was considered available for emergencies. Rabbi and Red therefore elected to land at Aslito — the first American planes to do so — to inspect the damage. They both put down successfully, but by that time it was too late in the evening to complete the inspection and get off the unlighted field.

During the night, the Japanese attempted to retake the field. It is more than a slight understatement to say that for a Naval Aviator, a fire fight on the ground is a somewhat novel experience. Later, Frog, Cap, and Fish Fischer also made use of the haven at Aslito. Indeed, Frog and Cap were there at the same time; Frog had a damaged right wing and Cap had a damaged left wing. With the help of an Army Air Forces master sergeant, they were able to switch Frog's good left wing for Cap's damaged left wing. This left Frog's plane as scrap but allowed the skipper to fly back to the carrier. Lieutenant Commander Butch Vincent retrieved Frog with a TBM.

Not all damage that was received over the islands was severe. I, too, was hit over Tinian. It was the only time that my aircraft was damaged either by the Japanese or by our own side. I was not even aware that the plane had been struck, but that evening after flight operations, I came onto the flight deck to cool off and my plane captain came over and said, "Mr. Smith, I have a souvenir for you." I was surprised and asked what it was. He said that as they were filling my plane's belly tank after its return to the carrier, they found gasoline running onto the flight deck. Inspection showed a leak in the belly tank, and a closer look produced a spent bullet that was then pried from where it was embedded in the tank. He offered me the mangled slug, but I told him that since he had found it, it was his to keep. To be honest, I really was not interested in having such a souvenir. That slug had come too close. My belief then and now is that bullets are best encountered as they depart and not as they arrive.

Our air patrols at this time encountered more Japanese search planes than at any previous time. The first incident occurred on 15 June, the day of the landings on Saipan, when one of the air group's TBMs on anti-submarine patrol sighted a twin-engine Japanese Betty. The Betty was at that period the standard land-based reconnaissance aircraft used by Japan and was the airplane believed responsible for the earlier bombing at Kwajalein. Our TBM was accompanied by an F6F flown by Charlie Lamb, who made several runs on the Jap and thoroughly riddled him. Indeed, Charlie had inflicted casualties and caused enough damage that not a single enemy gun was left functioning to return his fire. At about that time, the TBM torpedo bomber piloted by Hal Jedlund caught up with the action and blithely meandered alongside the crippled enemy to allow the turret gunner, Leon Bingham, to calmly administer the *coup de grace*. Poor Charlie took quite a ribbing on the carrier about letting a "pickle lugger" — torpedo bomber — pluck his pigeon.

Other later encounters by our fighter pilots during the Saipan operation produced better results. Lip and Kenneth "Monty" Montgomery each scored, downing Bettys. Lip got his while on CAP, and Monty scored while escorting Butch Vincent on an ASP. Later, Pardee "Corky" Finley dropped a Judy — the Japanese Yokosuka D-47, a single-engine, two-place reconnaissance plane. It was an unusual airplane for the Japanese in that the engine was a 12-cylinder inverted "V" type rather than a radial. These victories were good for squadron morale; a fighter pilot pictures himself as trained for aerial combat, and these were the first confirmed victories since the downing of the four-engine Mavis flying boat during the Tarawa operation.

The VF pilots were not the only ones who had scored on these patrols. On 19 June during an ASP, Gene Sabin and his crew in a TBM spotted a Japanese submarine on the surface and attacked. As the submarine dove, they laid a string of depth charges along its length from stern to bow. The attack was successful, and the *I-184*, commanded by Lieutenant Commander Matsuji Rikihasa was sunk (Orita and Harrington, 246). It is believed that this event made the *Suwannee* the first carrier to be responsible for sinking enemy submarines in both the Atlantic and Pacific theaters. In their official history of naval air operations during World War II, the Navy's Aviation History Unit observed, "The word 'invaluable' has perhaps become hackneyed in its constant association with our escort carriers, but they deserved the adjective in the Marianas, where their absence could only have prolonged the war" (206).

After a few days of heavy operation off Saipan, the *Suwannee's* AvGas supply was almost depleted, so the ship departed the operating area long enough to refuel from a tanker. On the day of the refueling, 20 June, normal routine was followed with a scheduled pre-dawn launching of CAPs and ASPs. Standard practice for night operations was to launch by catapult, and that is how the flights got into the air in the black of that June morning. The CAP called for 12 aircraft to patrol over the carriers at 15,000 feet. Atypically for this period, I was scheduled to fly wing on the skipper. There were six torpedo bombers on the ASP schedule, each with a 60-degree sector. On the morning of the launch, the torpedo bombers were catapulted first with the fighters following. The torpedo bombers proceeded into their search sectors while the fighters rendezvoused to make their patrol as a unit. The skipper was leading. After rendezvous, a climb was initiated toward patrol altitude. The flight was just passing 10,000 feet in the inky blackness when several pilots noticed a fire on the water at some distance to the west. Apparently the skipper had noticed the fire at about the same time, because he ceased the climb and started a let-down to investigate. At 1,500 feet, the flight was almost to the fire, which was still burning vigorously.

Without warning, the whole sky seemed to erupt with shell bursts. Intense yellow flashes appeared in large numbers all around. Though heavy antiaircraft fire was later experienced by many, no subsequent encounter ever equalled the severity met that June dawn. We did not learn until later that it was a U.S. fleet shooting at the flight. U.S. antiaircraft shells of that period exploded with a pronounced yellow color, while the Japanese shells exploded with a deep reddish-orange tint. Without delay, the skipper executed a turn to reverse direction. It was tough staying behind him, because the natural instinct of any sane human being is to depart from such an area as rapidly as his plane could carry him. The explanation of the fire on the water was that this trigger-happy fleet had downed a *Suwannee* ASP plane — the TBM of Lieutenant (jg) Paul Higginbotham with his crew, radioman Bill Barlow and ordnanceman Bob Wolfe.

All of the planes in our formation were equipped with IFF (Identification — Friend or Foe) gear, the precursor of the transponders that are currently in use today by civilian air traffic control. An IFF unit was designed to respond in code to interrogation by a radar search unit. The code changed from day to day with pilots being given the code at preflight briefing. Out of the 12 airplanes in our patrol that day, one or more of the IFF units certainly must have been functioning. I can only conclude that the fleet commander fired on the flight in spite of this indication of non-hostile status. I suspect that this type of incident resulted for the most part from nervous mistakes. At the time, however, it was difficult to be so broad-minded. This was the first, but certainly not the only, instance in which air group pilots were on the receiving end of fire from our own surface ships. Being fired upon always produced a strong urge to return the favor and shoot back. As far as is known, though, none of the carrier pilots ever succumbed to that temptation when they knew the firing was being done by our side.

Strikes in support of ground troops were controlled by experienced combat officers. Sometimes these controllers were on the ground and sometimes in the air. At that time the radio call sign of a controller was "Uncle" followed by a number. As the fighting on the ground shifted from place to place, one or another combat unit would find itself encountering difficulty from the Japanese. The unit would pass the word through chain of command to the appropriate Uncle controller. The strike aircraft would be in orbit on holding station with adequate bombs and ammunition, and the Uncle would call them with instructions as to where they should expend their ordnance. Sometimes the call required bombing as close as a hundred yards from our own front lines. Because of their long exposure to the pressures of the ground war, some of these controllers could be quite short-tempered and sarcastic, particularly so when a strike leader had trouble identifying the specific target or if the strike didn't demolish an assigned target.

One instance is particularly memorable. The assigned target was especially difficult to see. Finally, the lead plane in the formation, who was to make the first bombing run, thought he had the target spotted. This pilot called the Uncle station to say the target was identified as a tank at a set of coordinates, which the pilot read from a gridded map of the island. There followed a stream of profanity from the Uncle controller which included the information that that particular tank was sacrosanct because he was in it.

On the other hand, some of these controllers had a sense of humor and were not above giving a pat on the back for a job well done. One instance involved a flight of eight aircraft carrying 1,000-pound semi-armor piercing bombs who were on station over Tinian. The reason for carrying the semi-armor piercing bombs was not because of expectation of encountering a hardened target but because the ship had limited magazine capability and all of the general purpose bombs had been expended.

The flight of eight was called in by an airborne controller who had noticed that the Japanese had repaired the runway on one of the Tinian airstrips to make it operational. Instructions were to return the airstrip to non-operational status by judiciously pot-holing the runway. The planes pushed over — rolled and entered a dive — one by one from 10,000 feet. An airstrip is obviously a very big target and easy to hit, so no one felt obligated to carry a bomb to minimum release altitude. The eight fighters dropped their bombs with almost equal spacing on alternating sides of the runway along the full length. There was no way that a Japanese aircraft could weave its way around those holes to a successful takeoff or landing. The controller was quite pleased and didn't hesitate to say some nice things to the flight.

Air Group 60 was on the receiving end of plenty of ground fire during flights over Saipan and Tinian. Needless to say, there was no hesitation in returning this fire when it could be determined where it originated, but on both islands the Japanese soon learned not to use tracer ammunition, so it was often difficult to identify the source of their fire.

Every night, all hands were kept awake by being sent to general quarters because Japanese intruder aircraft regularly came down from the north. The long hours of flying combined with lack of rest at night took a toll on the aircrews. From my station on the after portion of the flight deck, I was in a position to see any action that occurred in connection with the nighttime intruders. Fortunately, most of our time off Tinian and Saipan occurred during the dark phase of the moon, so the Japanese aircrews couldn't get visual fixes on the ships; they were not helped much by their poor radar, either. Even so, they regularly found us. In the ebony-black nights, it was occasionally possible to glimpse the glow of their exhausts as they wandered across the sky above us.

One night I got a much better view of such a Japanese exhaust than I really wanted when one of the intruders flew across our ship barely above and forward of masthead height. Dacus and Kitzman (66-67) report that the Jap dropped a torpedo at a range too close for the torpedo to arm. They also give Lieutenant (jg) Premo, the navigator, credit for the maneuver that obviated any damage to the *Suwannee*. The Jap plane commander paid for his folly, because one of the destroyers in our screen shot him down. This destroyer was one of the new *Farragut* class with radar-controlled guns, and it had only recently joined our division. Not a shot had yet been fired, but this destroyer apparently had been tracking the intruder on radar, because suddenly there was a short burst from the destroyer's guns, followed by a streak of flame that arced across the sky and disappeared into the water. It looked like the work of a mad surrealist artist who had exchanged paint for fire. In a totally black night, the inky curtain was raised for a few seconds by a brilliant red fireball.

After spending several nights on the flight deck, I decided that if a bomb hit that portion of the ship I was a goner regardless of whether or not I was vertical or horizontal. I, therefore, climbed into the after portion of a TBM where a radioman would be stationed during flight. At this station there was a flat metal seat that was used by the crewman when he operated the radio or radar. The seat was wide enough to be comfortable for two people, and three could squeeze together uncomfortably. With appropriate bending I was able to lie down across this seat, and I promptly went to sleep. In the wee hours of the morning, after the Japanese had gone home, I awakened to find myself alone with all hands long hence secured from general quarters. That metal seat proved to be a torture rack — when I awoke every joint in my body ached. I never again repeated such a nocturnal sojourn in a TBM. Instead, I found other ways to steal a few winks.

I believe that the fatigue that accompanied the heavy flying schedule in combination with our loss of sleep contributed to the relatively large number of aircraft damaged by ground fire and the operational accidents that occurred during this period. One TBM went into the drink after a free-run takeoff. Fortunately, all of the crew got out and were picked up by a destroyer. Later, in the Philippines, Frog La Fargue also got wet when he dipped a wing after a wave-off from an aborted landing. Again, a destroyer came to the rescue and plucked our Arkansas rice farmer out of the sea.

During this period of close-air support in the Marianas, the Japanese navy decided it was time to stop the U.S. naval advance across the Central Pacific. They believed that the Marianas constituted the key to unlocking America's inner ring of defensive. The Japanese correctly believed that these islands had to be held in order to keep their home islands beyond the limits of long-range aerial bombardment. They hoped to make up for their limited supply of Japanese naval aircraft by bringing the Americans into battle west of Saipan but within range of land-based bombers flying from Guam, Yap, and Rota.

Early warning of an impending naval encounter came from our submarines. It was evident by 15 June 1944 that the Japanese carriers were sallying to engage our fast carrier force that was operating to the west of the

Marianas while the support carriers were operating to the east. What has become known as the Battle of the Philippine Sea was fought during the period 18 to 20 June 1944.

The Japanese in this engagement were strongly outnumbered with their 9 carriers opposing the American fleet of 15 fast carriers. In the annals of American naval aviation, this period has become known as the "Marianas Turkey Shoot," because a total of approximately 500 Japanese aircraft were shot from the air. The results of the battle were predictable. Little damage was done to the American fleet, but several Japanese carriers were sunk or severely damaged. This is the battle in which Admiral Marc Mitscher turned on the lights of the carrier fleet to save as many aircrews as possible when they were returning after dark on 20 June 1944. Even so, approximately 100 American aircraft were lost out of over 200 that were launched on that strike. The air groups of the support carriers, however, were stuck in our secondary role in defense of the invasion forces, and thus our air group missed the Turkey Shoot.

During the period of operation off Saipan and Tinian, one unusual flight was assigned. My logbook shows that it was on 24 June 1944 and involved the fighter squadrons from three air groups — the flight was an escort mission for a photo reconnaissance trip to Guam. Photos were to be taken by one of the TBMs from the *Suwannee*; the plane was to be flown by Frank Langdon and his crew. The escorting fighters were divided among several levels between 8,000 and 20,000 feet, and the photo plane was at one of the lower levels — possibly 8,000 feet, but my memory is not reliable here. The large formation passed north and south over Guam a number of times to obtain the desired pictures. Japanese antiaircraft fire was intense and sufficiently accurate to get a direct hit on one of the U.S. planes at 20,000 feet. The Japanese evidently received enough warning that the mission was inbound, because all of the Japanese aircraft had been flown away from the island to protect them from loss. An exception was a Hamp — a Mitsubishi A6M — that was shot down by one of the fighters from another ship. The Hamp was a variant of the famous Zero fighter. It was the same airplane as the Zeke, but the Hamp had square wingtips and the Zeke had round wingtips.

By early July 1944 the activity on Saipan was reduced. There was enough air support from shore based P-47s on Saipan plus a reduced number of CVEs to take care of the immediate requirements on Saipan and the later landings on Tinian. Accordingly, CarDiv 22's attention was shifted to Guam. The *Suwannee* was, therefore, relieved to proceed first on a quick trip to

Eniwetok to resupply stocks of almost everything from food to ordnance and spare parts. These stocks were approaching exhaustion.

Chapter 8

The Action Continues on Guam

THE *Suwannee* arrived at Eniwetok, and the air group remained aboard ship as she steamed into an anchorage. Normally, planes would fly ashore half a day or more ahead of the ship, but in this instance there was no reason for doing so as the stay was scheduled to be quite short. The entry and anchoring could be watched from one of the catwalks. Anchorage was within the lagoon of the coral island ring. The channel into the lagoon was relatively narrow but comfortably deep for the ship's entry; however, there were reefs on either side, and the ship had to be steered with care. Once in the lagoon, there were no charted hazards. As the ship proceeded inward, the depth increased appreciably and the calm water was a gorgeous azure blue — the prettiest ocean water I had seen during the entire cruise.

It wasn't long before lighters began to scurry forth from the shore to tie up alongside. Supplies began to pour aboard, including a very welcome load of mail. This provided a real boost in morale for everyone.

While in port, pilots aboard ship normally have little to do, and that was certainly true in this case. Any opportunity to get ashore was utilized gladly. Several pilots managed to join a liberty party and rode ashore in the ship's whale boat. The whale boat landed on the main island of Eniwetok, which is on the east side of the lagoon. The island was quite long and narrow. There was room for a single runway estimated to be 4,000 to 5,000 feet in length with either end terminating at the water's edge. Three or four rows of airplanes were parked on the lagoon side of the runway, so the width of the island must have been 150 to 200 yards in the widest region. At the north end of the runway, a segment of the island diverged from the direction of the runway and continued in a gentle arc to the west for a distance of perhaps one-quarter to one-half mile. On this northern portion a number of buildings had been constructed; both a CASU unit and a Navy patrol squadron were stationed there. The patrol squadron flew the Consolidated PB4Y Liberator, which was equivalent to the Army's B-24 four-engine bomber. The boys in the patrol squadron were quite friendly and offered to take some of us VF 60 pilots on a patrol with them; they even promised that our men could fly the planes. The offer was tempting, but the length of the squadron's routine patrol was 16 hours, and it was not known when our ship would leave. Regretfully, the offer was refused; it would have been extremely difficult to explain why we were on a joyride in a PB4Y instead of aboard a carrier departing to support an invasion of Guam. In the Naval Reserve in postwar years, I was able to fly a PB4Y, and the missed opportunity at Eniwetok was corrected. The PB4Y was a docile and comfortable machine and quite easy to land. The one negative impression I received from those postwar flights was that the rudder pressure necessary for cross-wind landings required the pilot to have well-developed leg muscles.

An exploration of Eniwetok was substituted for the missed patrol flight. Vegetation was sparse; you could almost count the bushes and trees. The absence of significant flora was not an endemic feature of the island environment but a result of the combination of the bombing and shelling the island had endured and the later runway construction. With regrowth of the vegetation, it could have become a retiree's paradise, but unfortunately the postwar atomic tests made it uninhabitable. The dearth of living organisms on the island made the surrounding reef a more attractive locus for investigation. This reef extended around the perimeter of the island and sloped gently outward in all directions. There was a wide variety of reef life including anemones, sea urchins, holothurians, and mollusks. Fish of various sizes and bright colors abounded. Wherever there was an available niche, some organism had adapted to fill it.

Later that afternoon, before the opening of the bar at the Officers Club on the northernmost tip of the island, a number of pilots went swimming. The water temperature was as ideal as the color of the lagoon. During that swim someone cornered and caught a small octopus. Back on the beach, after the O-Club opened, everyone had a few beers — excluding the octopus, of course. However, even he (or maybe she) got some benefit from the party, because bottles emptied quickly and the octopus crawled into one. It was impressive to see how the octopus could distort its shape to move in and out through the narrow neck, much like they do to get into narrow coral reef crevices.

During our day or two at Eniwetok, the squadron organization was again reshuffled, and I became a section leader with Corky as wingman. Our departure from Eniwetok was uneventful. Landings were scheduled to occur on Guam on 21 July, and logbook entries show that the air group was very busy there from the 12th through the rest of the month and into August.

After leaving Eniwetok, four additional officers, Marines, were aboard ship; they were to serve as flight controllers and to man the two Stinson L5 aircraft that had been loaded before leaving Espiritu Santo. These planes were stored with wings disassembled from the fuselages, and all components had been suspended from the I-beams that ran athwart ship above the hangar deck. One of these Marine officers was a major, and he was quartered with Dew, Red, and me. He was a hard character and by mid-1944 had been in the Pacific theater for over two years. Some of the stories that he told about the land fighting were hair-raising. It seems that, with rare exceptions, the fatalistic outlook of the Japanese fighting man was such that he would rather die than surrender. As a result, many Marines were killed or maimed by Japanese committing suicide while feigning surrender. Human nature is such that this engendered a rather strong antagonism, actually hatred, on the part of many young Marines. According to the major, the net result was that, even in those cases where a Japanese prisoner was taken, he might not make it to interrogation. It was not unusual for a Japanese prisoner being led to a rear area to be shot by a "stray bullet." This may sound shocking to the civilian who has not experienced the multiple brutal and useless deaths of a war.

Our Marine major and one of the other three Marine officers were to serve as flight controllers while we operated over Guam. They would fly in the TBMs, low and slow over the heavy fighting, to get a clear view before calling in strike aircraft. No one aboard ship envied the TBM crews. The greater speed and lesser maneuverability of the TBM when compared to the L5 combined to make the TBM inferior for the intended role. However, until there was a place for the L5s to operate, there was no option. The remaining two Marine officers served as pilots of the L5s, once the landings had progressed to the point that a sufficiently secure airstrip could be procured to support operation of the aircraft.

Pilot Bill Keller could attest to the fact that these flights were not "plum" assignments. A Japanese hit in the engine of his TBM had resulted in his plane — and everyone in it — getting a saltwater bath, including Keller and the Marine controller. Indeed, they were fortunate to have enough altitude and control to make it off the island. Ralph Hennings, the turret gunner, heroically pulled a stunned and half-drowned radioman, Stewart Neasham, from the belly of the plane before it sank. For those few days, the TBM pilots who flew the controllers very definitely earned the few extra dollars that Navy flight crews were awarded as extra hazard or flight pay. Fortunately, it was not long after Keller's dunking that a makeshift airstrip capable of operating the L5s was available, thanks to the Marine advance.

It was then that the ship lost its Marine contingent. The L5s were lowered from their suspension above the hangar deck and assembled. Then they were taken by elevator to the flight deck, which they had all to themselves because the ship's aircraft were all airborne. There was a good breeze over the flight deck as the ship turned into the wind, and the L5s were almost ready to fly with only the movement of the ship. Even so, they both took off using the full length of the deck in order to build a large excess of speed before going over the bow. Then each in turn did steep wingovers and flew just above the water on opposite course to the ship. They passed close aboard on the port side and waved up to those who were watching from the port catwalk.

One of these two L5 pilots had somewhere purchased an extra insurance policy — an iron lid off an old pot-bellied stove. He flew with this lid under him on the seat of his plane to act as a substitute for lack of armor plate. Apparently this worked satisfactorily because Lip has reported seeing him alive and well as a survivor of the war.

Guam was an exceptional operation in that the softening-up procedures that preceded the actual landings were a feint and conducted at a site on the opposite side of the island from the site of the actual landings. Of the two tenable locations for landings, one was on the southeast side of the island and one was in the middle of the west side in the vicinity of Apra Harbor, just above Orote peninsula. The feint was made on the southeast side; the actual landings were made at Apra after the Japanese forces had been lured to the other side of the island. As a result, the initial landings were relatively lightly opposed. This does not, of course, mean that light opposition continued indefinitely, because as soon as the Japanese moved their forces back across the island, the fighting was intense.

Aircraft from the *Suwannee* took their share of hits. The following accounts are undoubtedly not exhaustive but are representative of what was encountered.

Billie "Mac" McManemin was hit in his engine and was barely able to make it into the water west of Guam. He was so close to shore that, after inflating his rubber raft, he was within rifle range and had to paddle an appreciable distance to reach a depth sufficient for a rescue vessel to retrieve him. Ed "Fish" Fischer took a 40-millimeter round through one of his propeller blades. Fortunately, the shell did not explode, but it left a large, round hole through the central axis of the blade. The outer and inner sections of the blade were held together by narrow strips of metal along the leading and trailing edges. Had the two sections of the blade parted, the rotational imbalance would have torn the engine out of the plane. The hole did generate a unique sound; his eerie propeller whine announced his approach to the ship far in advance of his appearance in the "groove."

Donald "Pappy" Knapp was hit in the wing root by a shell, probably a 40-millimeter, that did explode. The hole was quite pronounced and made his return to the ship rather touchy. His flaps were not functional, and his hydraulic line was ruptured, so that before landing, he had to use his dump bottle — filled with compressed nitrogen to pressurize the hydraulic system — to lower his landing gear.

The torpedo bombers also took their hits. Paul "Geltchy" Golsh and his crew in a TBM were hit in the after belly section with a shell that exploded. Both Howard Booz, the gunner, and Claude Park, the radioman, were injured, the latter very seriously. In spite of his own injuries, Booz attended to Park and kept him from bleeding to death by fashioning a tourniquet from a microphone cord. Golsh diverted with a fighter escort to the Aslito airstrip on Saipan where Park was given immediate medical attention. He was subsequently airlifted to Pearl Harbor while Golsh and Booz returned to the ship.

Flight schedules at this time were heavy; my logbook shows that two flights a day were not uncommon. In a single day, on 15 July, I logged 8.7 hours from a combination of a CAP and a strike. As a result, pilot fatigue was still a problem. In one instance, a TBM did not stay airborne after a free-run (non-catapult) takeoff because the pilot pulled up too sharply. There were no injuries, and by the grace of the fates, all three of the crew were picked up.

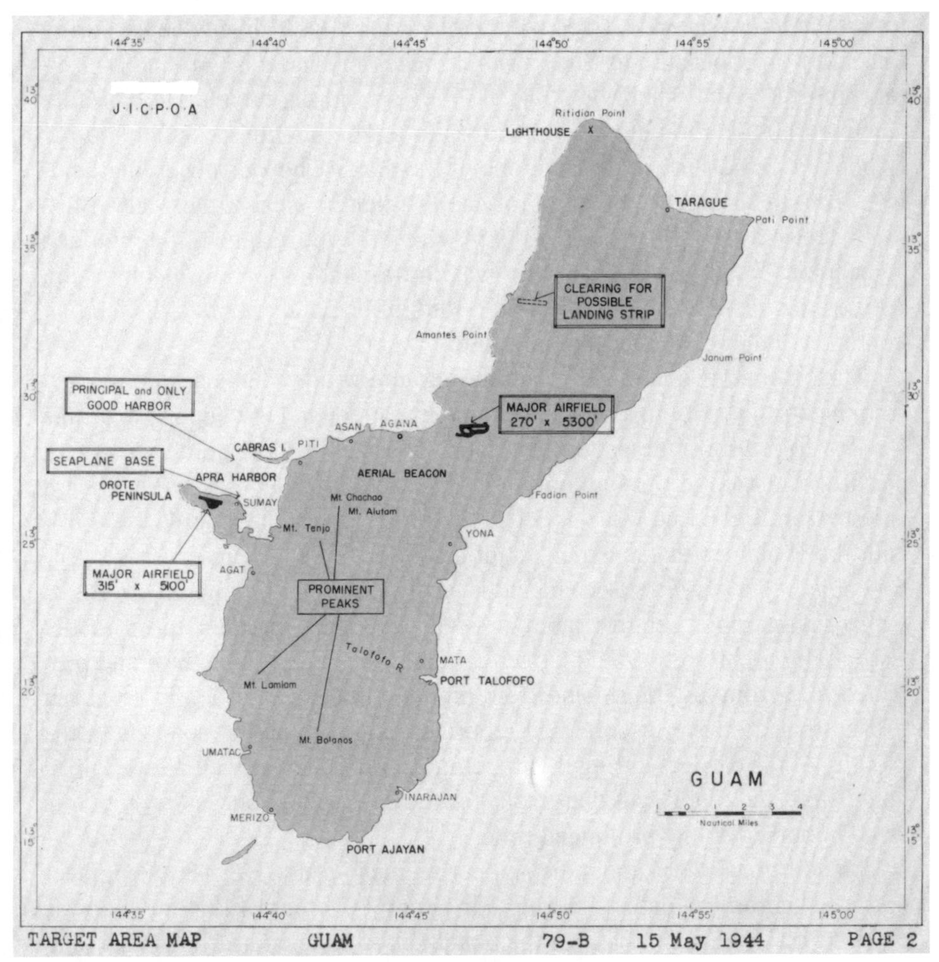

The island of Guam. Objects of interest to pilots are highlighted.

On the VF side, both Frog La Fargue and Rabbi Shea went into the water during aborted landings. Frog was rescued by the USS *Kidd*, and his story is well told in Dacus and Kitzman's *As We Lived It*. Frog visited the *Kidd* years later at the Louisiana War Memorial where the ship is berthed and confirmed the rescue from her log. Rabbi's story is also interesting. When he hit the water, his left wing impacted first, causing the plane to knife downward. As Shea later gave a firsthand account, he was rigged for a carrier landing with the canopy open and harness unstrapped. Thus with the release of his safety belt and the unplugging of his radio earphones, his egress from the plane took only a few seconds. Even so, the plane must have dived deeply during that short time, because as Shea swam to reach the surface he found himself reaching the point where he could no longer hold his breath. He therefore triggered both carbon dioxide cartridges to inflate his life jacket and quickly popped to the surface. Indeed, one of the pilots who was observing landings from the bridge said that he rose so fast that he cleared the water by 10 to 15 feet before falling back. This may be a slight exaggeration, but Red Rynearson, Rabbi's wingman who was in the landing pattern behind him, verifies that he rose clear of the water. Red immediately aborted his landing approach and circled over the pilot in the water.

The *Suwannee* continued steaming into the wind, which carried it away from its normal station. The ship became impatient and issued repeated calls for Red to return to the pattern and land. These calls were politely ignored, and Red returned to the ship only after his section leader was safely aboard a destroyer. When Red was queried afterward as to why he ignored the ship's calls, he explained that a man in an inflated Mae West life preserver is a very tiny object in a very large ocean and is easily lost in a running sea. To Red's way of thinking, keeping Rabbi in sight seemed a prudent thing to do. Essentially all aircrew would agree; certainly the skipper bought it and protected Red from any reprimand from higher authority. But he did point out to Red that destroyer escorts had reported many submarine contacts in the vicinity of the carriers during their operations off Guam as well as off Saipan and Tinian and that it was dangerous for the carriers to unnecessarily hold a steady course for any prolonged time.

An additional word about the skipper seems in order. He was an engineer and was taciturn by nature. During Air Group 60's tour of sea duty, he was working on a gun sight that was the precursor of the modern "heads-up" display. He had a great depth of knowledge about the F6F, particularly its efficient operation and the strengths and limitations of its various components. On one occasion, he was able to keep an F6F in the air for over eight and a half hours. He was very much interested in the combat readiness and safety of his pilots. I can cite two of my own experiences off Guam to illustrate his interest in safety. In the first instance, my tail hook extended partially during a catapult launch. After rendezvous, my wingman radioed that the hook was partially extended. I nodded to him to indicate that I heard and immediately placed the switch in retract position. I got a green light to indicate the hook was in, but I made no radio transmission. It was the wingman's transmission that brought the problem to the attention of the skipper, who happened to be monitoring the frequency. The skipper notified the ship's control center that I was not to be brought aboard until he okayed it, because he feared that the hook would jam in its track during subsequent extension. If the hook did not extend fully, it could easily pull free when a landing wire was engaged and thus allow me to continue forward into a barrier crash.

When our flight returned to the ship, the skipper was on the ship's radio and queried me as to the hook's status. I told him that I had my selector in the down position and had a green light; however, he said that because the initial catapult acceleration had induced the extension, the green light was not a positive indication. He asked my load status. I informed him that my belly tank was dry, but I had 3,600 rounds of ammunition because there had been no occasion to expend it. He immediately ordered me to fly well clear of the ships and fire this ammunition to lighten the aircraft. While I was doing as instructed, the ship took the rest of the flight aboard. They called me and told me to expedite getting rid of the 50-caliber rounds. I obeyed, though I was reluctant to fire bursts that were too long or too close together. However, they were in a hurry because they were steaming on the windline, which was not the track they wanted to make. As it turned out, I came aboard uneventfully—the hook held without any problem. I told the ordnance officer that I thought the gun barrels had become very hot and that they should be checked carefully. I found that the barrels were, indeed, damaged, and the escapade cost the Navy six new ones. The skipper later told me that had I informed him that the hook retracted satisfactorily, he would have known that the mechanism was undamaged. However, the mechanism was such that had I been unable to retract it but could still extend it from a midpoint position, the hook might be improperly seated in its track and result in a failure during arrested landing.

The second incident cost the Navy a belly tank and 150 gallons of gasoline. The flight was scheduled for only two or three hours instead of the normal four or five. This may have been the "milk run" to Rota, but at this point in time I am not sure. At any rate, the droppable belly tanks were not supposed to be filled, and at briefing we were told that they were empty. Launching proceeded in the usual manner, and we went our way. When we were some distance from the ship, I thought I heard the ship trying to make radio contact with me. The signal was so weak that I could easily have been mistaken. I turned up the volume and listened intently, but there was nothing further. I concluded that my hearing had been faulty. When we returned to the ship and prepared to land, I was asked via my radio if I had burned fuel from my belly tank. I answered that I had not because that tank was supposed to be empty, and any attempt to draw on an empty tank could cause a vapor lock. I was told that the belly tank on my plane had been filled by mistake, and I was ordered to jettison the tank immediately. Later, when back aboard, the skipper explained that the mounting brackets for the drop tank were adequately strong to withstand the rapid acceleration of a catapult takeoff with a full tank, but the bracing was wrong for the deceleration of an arrested landing. A carrier landing with a full drop tank could cause the tank to break free and travel forward through the propeller. The attendant rupture of the tank would almost certainly result in a nasty fire. I found out later that such events actually had happened on other carriers.

In the later phases of the operations, first on Saipan and Tinian and then on Guam, there were often times when the Uncle controllers had no immediate targets for the available planes. Under those circumstances, pilots were released to hunt for "targets of opportunity." This gave the freedom to attack anything that looked useful to the Japs. As might be expected, our choices weren't always correct. In one instance, a chicken coop was blown to smithereens — but at least this must have reduced the food supply. On another occasion, a pilot found a shed that he thought might be used for the storage of ammo or materiel. He was carrying a 500-pound general purpose bomb with a ten-second delay fuse. He skip-bombed that baby right into the shed. When he circled back, he couldn't find anything to indicate that that shed had ever existed. It must have been an empty sugar cane storage structure.

On Guam, I almost shortened some coconut trees at the end of Agana airstrip one afternoon while hunting a worthwhile target, preferably a hidden airplane. I made a fast pass down the airstrip just above the ground looking from side to side to see if anything was hidden under the trees. It's amazing how short a runway can be at that speed; when I again looked forward, the coconut grove off the end of the runway was very close. Instinctively, I pulled back on the stick and to this day remain convinced that the palm fronds at the top of the coconut grove were set swaying by propwash.

These "hunting expeditions" were not all innocuous. One day Corky Finley and I found a Japanese gun emplacement on the steep western slope of a hilly portion of the island just south of Apra Harbor. It is hard to be sure from the air, but the caliber of the gun was estimated at three to five inches. The gun had sufficient range to keep shipping in its vicinity well off shore; it was also well defended with light antiaircraft weaponry. To make a run at the emplacement from the sea would give their gunners a "no deflection" shot and would be asking for trouble. We, therefore, elected to make a steep drop down the side of the hill where the contour allowed the approach to be shallowed during the latter portion of the run to provide reasonably accurate strafing. Recovery could then be made seaward while doing evasive maneuvers. Fortunately, a little puffball cloud was hanging a few hundred feet above the crest of the hillside. The attacks could be hidden by starting behind this cloud and then dropping down to be well into the approach before the Jap gunners could see the planes. We made several such strafing attacks until return fire ceased. Back on the ship, we reported the gun's position in the debriefing session. Because the gun emplacement endangered shipping entering the harbor, it seems sure that either a bombing flight later paid an unfriendly visit to the site or the heavier ships at sea shelled the site to nullify its utility.

Other targets were potentially even more lethal. Tex Garner ran into one near Marpi point on Saipan. He strafed a likely looking cave that apparently was an ammo dump, for it literally blew him "sky high." It was a good thing the F6F was such a rugged airplane; Tex's bird remained flyable. Most strafers saw or experienced similar events. On Guam, Willie Schmall also had an encounter with an ammo dump. He was strafing a camouflaged area without realizing what it was, and it blew up right in front of him. He later described his passage over where the dump had exploded as passing through a solid wall of acrid, black smoke with debris flying outward in all directions. Again, his survival attests to the quality products produced by the Grumman "Iron Works."

Support work on Guam wasn't flawless, however. There was an instance where the first flight in the morning was given coordinates to bomb. The flight went forth and hit exactly where it had been told with 500-pound general purpose bombs. This was pretty much routine practice. That evening, after all pilots were assembled in the ready room, the squadron intelligence officer entered with a dejected look on his face. He said, "I've got bad news for you fellows. The Marines moved up during the night, but there was a snarl-up in communications and word didn't get back. As a result, you hit the target exactly as it was given to you, but it was 200 yards behind the Marine front line." You could have heard the proverbial pin drop. What can you say when you've done what you are told to do and it is wrong? No one has yet succeeded in rolling back a page of time to erase a past event, so you can only continue to do a job to the best of your ability.

It seems worth noting that the ships were always interested in protecting themselves and were not always at the location that was expected from the information at preflight briefing. One day a flight was returning from its scheduled activity and a heavy line squall toward the east could seen.

The F6F Hellcat on the flight deck. (Photo, Grumman Corp.)

Briefing information would have put the carriers in the clear on the flight's side of the squall, but the ships were not there. The flight leader called, reported the conditions, and requested a radar steer. The *Suwannee* answered that it was in a region of highly restricted visibility and was unable to take planes aboard. The flight was advised to remain clear of the clouds and to hold its present position. It was obvious that the ships had run under the squall to hide themselves from discovery by enemy aircraft. The carrier again called after several minutes to say it was finally in the clear, and the flight was allowed to come in on a heading that was specified. The planes dropped to a level just above the water and flew inbound. The farther they flew the thicker the weather became. The pilots could barely see from one plane to the next. After a period of time, the ship again came on the VHF

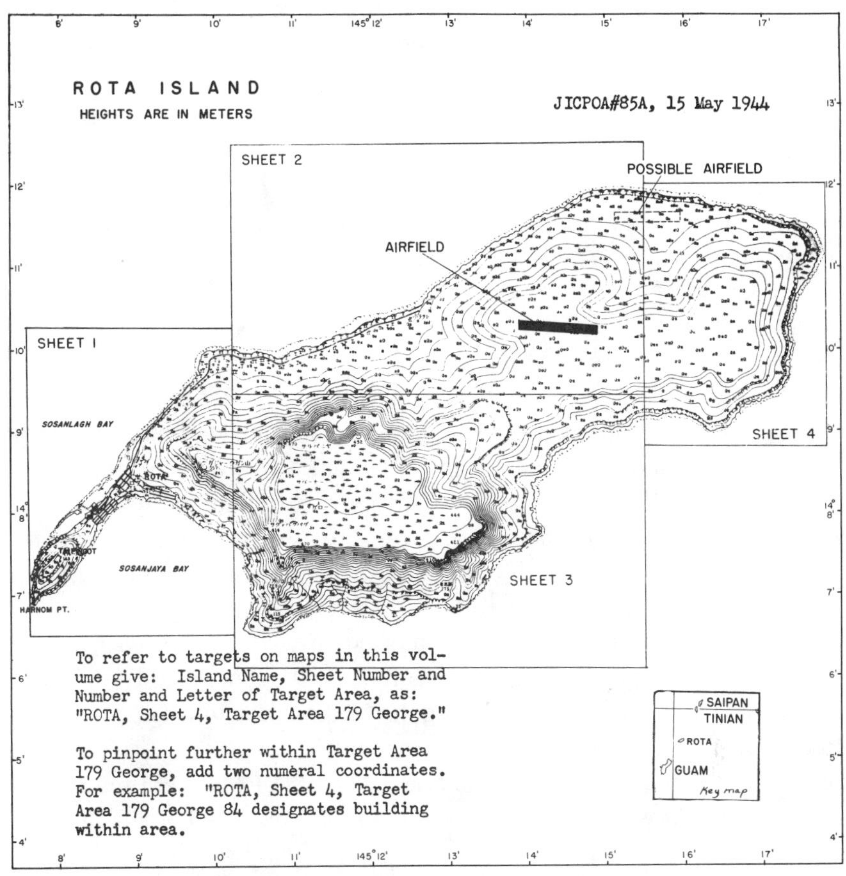

The objective on Rota, the target of the "milk run."

radio and gave a rather minor change in heading. To hear that transmission was encouraging because it meant that the ship and planes were sufficiently close together to be within line of sight, which at this low level meant within a distance of five to ten miles. The flight flew on for what seemed an inordinate amount of time when the outermost plane of the second division came on the radio and said he had spotted a ship's wake at a relative bearing of three o'clock.

The flight leader promptly turned and followed the wake, and it was not too long before the flight passed one of the destroyers in the carrier screen. The destroyer's position in combination with the wakes from other ships was used to find the *Suwannee*, where the flight orbited at masthead height. When the ship was ready to take planes aboard, formation was broken from this abnormally low altitude, and pilots had trouble keeping track of each other and the ships during the landing procedure. The debriefing officer was told that it was the pilots' fervent hope that they would never again be forced to land aboard when the ships were "in the clear." The sourpuss didn't even laugh, but then he had not flown in that thick glop.

One incident in connection with Guam that stands out was a replenishment trip that the *Suwannee* made to Saipan. During the periods of heavy operation, ordnance and AvGas could rapidly be expended. Replenishment at sea was the most frequent method of resupply, particularly for AvGas. A tanker would cruise alongside, lines would be passed across, and the tanker would pump fuel from their bunkers to ours. Transferring bombs at sea was a much trickier and more tedious operation and was avoided when possible. It was because of this that a run was made back to Saipan. Very little time was wasted from flight operations because of the proximity of Saipan to Guam. The ship maneuvered to the north during the day, and by late afternoon when the "milk run" to Rota was launched, the ship was very near Saipan. This "milk run" was accomplished just after dawn each day and again in the evening. The purpose was to keep the airstrip at Rota inoperative and was done almost daily during the Guam operation. The Japanese on Rota finally gave up filling the craters, but the air group didn't cease its harassment. Thus, on the day of interest, when the Rota flight returned and was recovered, it was less than an hour to the assigned anchorage off Saipan.

The anchorage was the channel between Saipan and Tinian. The stench from Saipan was strong even at the distance of the anchorage from the island, and a cargo of flies accumulated from the island tenaciously stayed aboard and pestered the crew for more than a week of steaming at sea. The invasion of Tinian was in progress and was being given air support from the airfields on Saipan, which were by then fully operational. The invasion was also being supported by battleships and cruisers that were anchored closer to Tinian than was the *Suwannee*. Our view of the shelling was from the breech side looking toward the direction of their fire. It was surprising to actually see the projectiles leave the barrels of the heavy rifles and watch part of their travel.

This may be explained by recognizing that the projectile from a 16-inch rifle weighs about 2,400 pounds, approximately as much as a modern Volkswagen. The *Suwannee* replenished overnight and was off again the next morning in time to launch the "milk run" to Rota. When the air group finally left the Mariana Islands, it was with regrets only for those who had been lost and not for the odor of decaying flesh that emanated from the island of Saipan.

The air group had anticipated rotation back to the States after the Marianas operations, but that was not to be. Indeed, we were to participate in two more operations before going stateside. One of them was to include the convergence of the air group, carrier, and kamikazes over the Philippine Deep. Before the next operation, Hal Jedlund was transferred out of the VT squadron, and Tim Casey and Jimmy Dunn came aboard to replace him and Paul Higginbotham.

Chapter 9

Morotai and Halmahera: The Dutch East Indies

CARDIV 22 was relieved to leave the Marianas the first week of August 1944. The first stop was Eniwetok for three days where "war-weary" planes were traded for replacements. These replacement aircraft proved to be no jewels. Whether the problems were due to shoddy workmanship in that particular CASU or to the abrasive nature of the coral dust on Eniwetok is unknown, but almost every one of those aircraft gave trouble before *Suwannee's* maintenance crews got things rectified during a two-week stay at the next port of call, the Admiralties. Shore-based facilities were available there. Without those maintenance people, a great many of the aircrews would not have come back. The aircrews appreciated those hard-working mechanics and riggers. They toiled long and often thankless hours, but they did a magnificent job. Arrival at the Admiralties was four days out of Eniwetok. A second passage of Truk occurred during this transit, but this time only a two-plane CAP was kept aloft instead of the CAP of three air groups during the passage in March. The war was changing rapidly.

During this sojourn in the Admiralties, aircrews were quartered in Quonset huts on the west end of the islet of Pitylu, only a short walking distance from the islet's airstrip. Toilet facilities were quite sanitary and were built on piers extending over the water. The toilets themselves consisted of long wooden seats with several suitable orifices. A roof overhead kept dry those who were using the premises. An absence of walls or railings on these open-air facilities allowed any occupant the opportunity to use his time watching colorful fish, squid, and other denizens of the reef in their natural environment. The squid were particularly attractive. They always appeared in groups and maneuvered in formation. Especially impressive was the rapidity with which all life could become quiescent and disappear when one or more predatory fish loomed. As a corollary to these fancy "outhouses," it is worth noting that human feces floats on salt water. As a result, swimmers had to be careful when timing their entry into the water along the western extremity of the islet to be sure that the tide was running out rather than in. Anyone entering the water during the wrong phase of the tide was wise to use the breast stroke to sweep away all foreign matter ahead of him. Luckily, this wasn't too much of a problem because the Admiralties are located in one of those unusual positions where the period of separation between flood and ebb tides is about 12 hours instead of 6.

The two weeks at Pitylu provided diversions. Herbie Beckerdite decided he would like to fly a TBM. He obtained one from the Pitylu CASU by promising to fly the base chaplain to and from Ponam, another islet on the barrier reef, to say Sunday Mass. I imparted my vast single-flight knowledge of the TBM's flight characteristics to Herbie and showed him how to start the monster. Fortunately, Herbie is a very gifted soul when it comes to airplanes, and with his talent and the grace of God they got there and back with the padre none the wiser about his novice pilot.

A particular highlight of the stay on Pitylu was that Bob Hope arrived and put on a USO show. It was a breath of fresh air. The group included Jerry Colonna as "second banana," Frances Langford as the singer, and Patty Thomas as a dancer. There was the usual chorus line of feminine pulchritude. Some of the air group bumped into Hope at the O-Club on Manus later in the day and found him to be as witty off the stage as on.

One story that needs to be told about Pitylu has to do with Bill Harrington's and my shell-collecting expeditions on the reef. At high tide, the reef had to be reached by swimming. Thick-soled Marine-issue shoes, known as "boondockers," were worn on the reef to protect the feet, and these were heavy enough to make swimming tiresome. And the heavy shoes compounded by an adverse current made it difficult to transport the collected shells back to the islet. Bill ingeniously solved the problem by carrying an empty sock to the reef. After he had stuffed the sock with desirable specimens, he tied it to that masculine appendage that has no function during swimming. Thus, all arms and legs were free to propel him to the shore. While at Pitylu, Bill received orders to report to Photographic Interpretation School in Washington, D.C., so when the ship left harbor he stayed behind to await transportation to the States. A letter from him from Washington said that he had taken a number of shells and beetles from our collecting expeditions to the Smithsonian Institution for their experts to examine. Among these were several species new to science, which the Smithsonian kept.

The flying schedule at Pitylu was not heavy. There was some aerial gunnery on high-speed — 180 to 200 knot — banners that were towed by twin-engine Lockheed PVs. One flight on the schedule was novel in that the whole air group rendezvoused with a departing U.S. submarine. This sub was proceeding from the Admiralties to its assigned patrol area and had been requested to dive and surface a couple of times after reaching deep water to demonstrate to the air group personnel how this maneuver appeared from the air. The vast majority of the pilots had never seen a submarine in actual operation at sea. The whole thing went off quite smoothly.

The air group flew back aboard ship on 29 August 1944, and the men found that they were on the way to the Dutch East Indies. Memory indicates that en route to this destination an event occurred aboard the *Sangamon* that illustrated one of the major hazards of routine day-to-day flight operations aboard a duty carrier. In late afternoon, a Hellcat was coming aboard. Whether the pilot was too high, too fast, or simply didn't chop his power in time is unknown, but the landing Hellcat floated over the barriers and crashed into a group of airplanes parked on the forward end of the *Sangamon's* flight deck. A fire ensued, along with personnel casualties, and several aircraft were destroyed. From the deck of the *Suwannee*, a group of men had watched this happen. There was a sense of utter frustration because, though only a short distance away, the men on the *Suwannee* might as well have been on another planet. There was absolutely no way to cross the intervening water to render assistance.

Two of my experiences during the interval between Eniwetok and Morotai in the Dutch East Indies serve to illustrate the sort of events that occasionally spiced up the tedium of orbiting for four or five hours on a routine CAP. One day, while relatively far from any significant Japanese base, Corky and I were on a two-plane CAP. The ship's radar picked up an unidentified blip near the limit of the radar's range. Our two F6Fs were immedi-

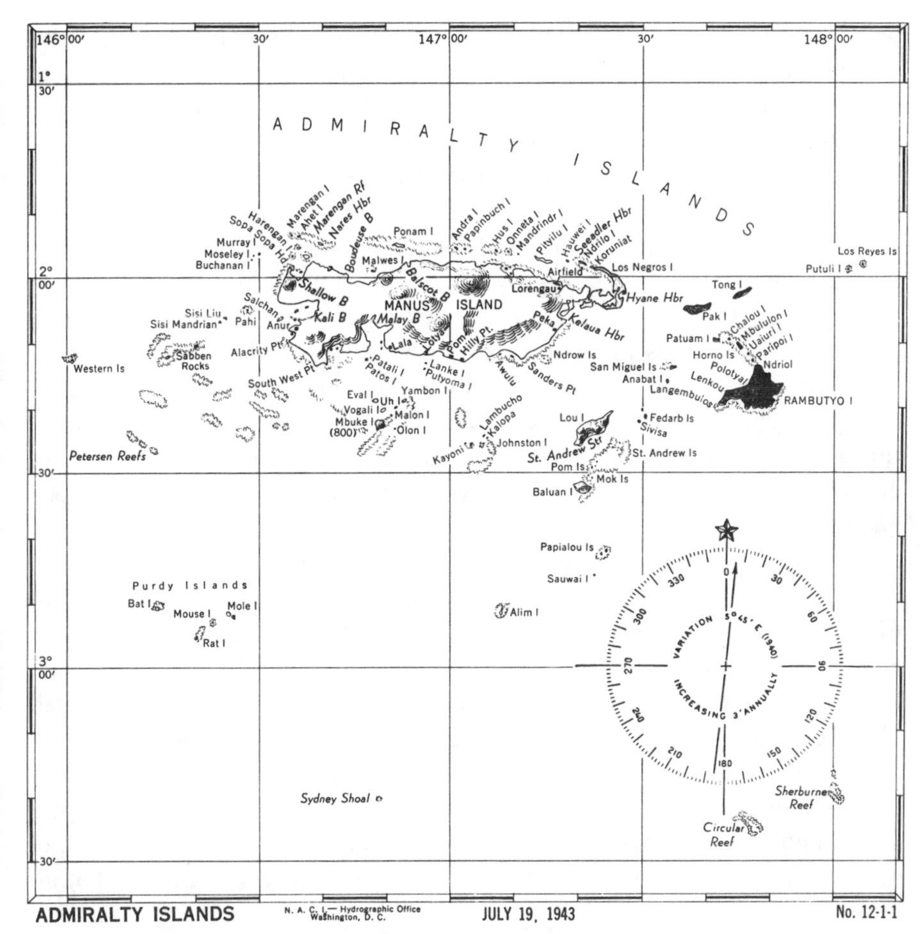

The Admiralty Islands showing the large island of Manus, approximately 60 miles long, with its barrier reef to the north containing the islets of Pitylu and Ponam.

ately vectored to intercept. By the time we got to where the blip had been, it had disappeared, and there was only blue sky. The ship decided that it was fruitless to hunt around at that distance, so the flight was ordered back to station. The monotony of the prolonged orbiting prior to the vector combined with a fruitless 100-mile trip to a nonexistent target left me disappointed and bored. Therefore, while inbound still 50 miles from the ship, I decided to do a few rolls. I signaled my intentions to Corky, who moved away. I then executed a long, lazy, slow roll. Upon completion, I found that my engine was no longer running. I had forgotten that I was drawing fuel from my belly tank. The fuel intake in that tank was at the low point, so when I was inverted, this intake was above the fuel level and was sucking in fumes. Had I been drawing from any one of the three internal tanks, there would have been no problem because of the dual inlets in those tanks. However, I had a vapor lock — a condition where the fuel flow between the tanks and the engine is broken by the presence of gaseous fumes. Because fuel pumps are designed to pump liquid and not gas, this leads to fuel starvation in the engine and a quiet ride for the pilot! The roll was undertaken at an altitude well above 10,000 feet. I switched tanks, used the auxiliary pump, and tried a number of other things. I was dropping through 5,000 feet and contemplating an uncomfortable ride in the life raft a long way from help when the engine finally caught and ran. There was never a sweeter sound nor such a beautiful sight as that ocean receding as the plane climbed away. The obvious conclusion was that there were better ways to break the tedium of a dull afternoon.

On another day, again when the carriers were in mid-ocean, Corky and I were on another two-plane CAP. Again the ship's radar picked up an unidentified blip, and we were vectored to intercept. There was a heavy cloud cover, and visibility was poor. However, the radar controller was good and he brought us close to the bogey in good attack position. I got an initial glimpse of an aircraft below and to the side as I passed from one cloud to another. Soon there was another fleeting glimpse of the bogey, and from the two sightings, the direction of travel could be ascertained. Corky and I split apart to place ourselves on either side and ahead of the bogey. That way, no matter which way the stranger turned, one of us would get a clear shot at him.

I soon got another and longer glimpse. The plane looked like a Japanese Betty; Corky agreed. Guns were charged and belly tanks dropped. When the unknown plane cleared the next cloud, gunnery runs were initiated. I was well into the run when I got my first clear look and quickly identified the unknown as a friendly B-24 or PB4Y. I immediately called Corky with the identification and told him to hold his fire and safety his guns. We continued our gunnery runs, by then simulated rather than actual, and passed in quick succession behind the intruder's tail. I passed from right to left and Corky from left to right. That crew was brought rudely awake. The intent was to let them know that there were other friendly forces in the area and that they should be running with their IFF gear operating to facilitate radar identification.

The reason for proceeding to the Dutch East Indies was to support a landing by Army forces on the island of Morotai, which is roughly ovate in shape, approximately 30 miles in length from south to north, and about 15 to 20 miles across from east to west. It is one of the easternmost islands of the East Indies and lies generally north of the much bigger island of Halmahera, which is quite irregular in shape. Its northwestern peninsula lies within ten miles of the southwestern coast of Morotai.

While en route to these islands, a rather extensive briefing was given about the peoples and history of the East Indies by Army intelligence officers who had been brought aboard solely for that purpose. The gist of what they said was that if a downed flier should be discovered by the natives, he should immediately make it clear that he wished to be taken to the village chief, the *Kapella Kampong*. It was felt that the flier was much more likely to receive protection and humane treatment at the hands of the chief than otherwise.

To facilitate a downed flier's interactions with members of the native population, each aircrewman was issued a packet of Dutch currency before each flight. Not a great deal of money was involved; my recollection is that it was equivalent to somewhere between $50 and $100. However, careful records were kept to see that each of these packets was returned during debriefing after each flight. The pilots were also issued a beautiful set of colored silk maps capable of withstanding saltwater immersion. These maps contrasted with the rubberized cloth maps that had been issued during earlier operations, though both showed prevailing patterns of wind and ocean currents in relation to the land masses in the region in which flight operations were to be conducted.

Early one evening during this voyage, a cluster of people on the forward end of the flight deck were gazing at something in the distance. When I looked in the direction of their gaze, I could see two tall columns of water extending from the ocean surface up into a localized cloud base. These were water spouts, swirling masses of white water. Water spouts and tornadoes are equivalent except that the former occurs over water and the latter over land. Also, tornadoes normally have funnel shapes while these water spouts had essentially the same cross-section from top to bottom. One of the ship's officers in the group commented that these phenomena were not uncommon in the waters through which the ships were cruising. He also noted that, over open water, they tended to occur in pairs with each spinning opposite to the other. These comments may have been authentic or only old sailor's tales.

One untoward event occurred aboard the *Suwannee* on the way to Morotai involving one of the plane captains. During wartime, it was normal for all ships to run under rigid blackout conditions with no external lights of any kind. Should a light be seen by any ship in the fleet, even for a short period of time, the Admiral was notified. He in turn would issue a reprimand to the Officer of the Deck on the offending ship. Night security watches on the flight deck were rotated among the junior officers of the air group. When standing these watches on clear nights, the stars sparkled and the constellations could be seen in great detail. On moonless nights, meteors literally blazed across the sky. In equatorial latitudes you could simultaneously see Ursa Major pointing to the north star, the Southern Cross, Scorpio, and Orion, the four corners of the sky. On one particularly dark night with cloud cover preempting even the starlight, a routine pre-dawn launching of a combat air patrol and an anti-submarine patrol was scheduled. When planes were manned, it was discovered that one of the plane captains was missing from his station in the last row on the flight deck. Because of the darkness, no one actually saw what had happened to him, but it is known that he came on deck to ready his assigned plane for flight. It is also known that it was his habit to make his way aft by counting the arresting wires that he passed; he used this count to stop at the row containing his aircraft. It seems almost certain that he missed a wire because of the darkness and walked right off the aft end of the flight deck. During scheduled flight operations there is no fencing of any kind around the flight deck, so that as you proceed toward the edge, the deck is there and then it isn't. When the flight was launched, a search was flown in the early dawn. The planes remained close above the water and retraced the carrier's passage. Regrettably, no sign of the captain was found.

CarDiv 22 arrived on station approximately 100 miles east of Morotai during the night of 14 September 1944. Pre-dawn on 15 September, strikes were launched against the Lolobata airstrip on Halmahera. Shortly after arrival there a *Santee* plane was hit and the pilot parachuted into Wasile Bay close to the Japanese shore. The pilot's rubber raft had apparently been damaged by the hit and was not serviceable. Fish Fischer of VF 60 recognized the problem and dropped his own raft to the man, who managed to get it inflated and climb in. However, he was close enough to shore to be under fire from the Japs. Strafing by American planes distracted the enemy while the downed pilot maneuvered to tie to the anchor chain of an old schooner located offshore; its hull offered some protection from the Japanese fire. The carriers sent successive groups of replacement fighters to keep up the strafing distraction throughout the day. Attempts by the Japs to reach the downed pilot by boat were thwarted. On the other hand, an attempt to rescue the pilot by a Dumbo, an air-sea rescue PBY flying boat, was frustrated by the heavy fire from shore. The actual rescue was accomplished by one of two PT boats that had been sent for that purpose. One of these PTs, with the aid of a smoke screen from a VT 60 TBM, made a daring run to the anchor chain and picked up the *Santee* pilot. The skipper of that PT boat was given the Medal of Honor for this exploit.

During the course of the strafing operations at Lolobata, VF 60 lost two planes and one pilot, Bill "Slim" Bannister. Frog La Fargue flew on that mission and saw the conditions under which Bannister was shot down. Frog said that Slim was trying to make a message drop to the downed *Santee* pilot and in the process was so low and close to the Jap guns that they did not miss. His plane impacted the water at high speed, and Slim never surfaced. The other Hellcat that was lost by VF 60 was flown by Paul "Big Red" Lindskog. In his case, the Jap antiaircraft fire ruptured his oil line, but he had enough power and control to ditch well away from shore. A PBY Dumbo was called and had no trouble in effecting a water landing and rescue; Big Red was then taken to Morotai. On the island, there were only a limited number of Japanese, so the action was not too spectacular. Thus the press who were covering the invasion needed some spice. Apparently, VF 60's young birdman spun some good yarns for them when he was interviewed. However, when he came back aboard ship he didn't seem to have too many regrets about leaving Morotai. It seems the island was somewhat less than a paradise.

The day of 16 September began, as did many other days, with the steward bending over my bunk and saying softly, "Mr. Smith, Suh! You have the pre-dawn hop." In tropical seas, it seemed to be always warm and humid, so we awakened somewhat groggy. When rolling out, our bare feet found the steel deck to be warm and clammy. Pilots wandered down the passageway to the head (toilet) and completed the morning ablutions. Individually, we went to the wardroom to join other pilots on the schedule for a quick breakfast that consisted, as usual, of a scrambled blob made from dehydrated powdered eggs and some rather muscular coffee. Indeed, before three o'clock in the morning, Navy coffee was always strong, so much so that many pilots would have hesitated to drop a nail into it for fear that the nail would dissolve. Most ate, however, because they knew that they wouldn't get anything more before noon, which was more than nine hours away. After breakfast, pilots convened in the ready room to don flight gear and be briefed for the hop. The first mission on 16 September called for a 12-plane CAP along the southern shore of Morotai, the site of the invasion.

At the briefing, information was given concerning the carrier's current latitude and longitude, anticipated ship's movements and location to be expected on return, pertinent survival information, and data concerning the status of the invasion with the enemy responses. Among other bits of information was the fact that the destroyers in the screen had again made sonar contact during the night with a shadowing submarine, but the screen had been effective in preventing any penetration for attack.

When the squawk box gave the command for pilots to man their planes, we dutifully proceeded from the ready room through a passageway where each pilot grabbed and donned his parachute harness with its survival pack in the back. The lights in the ready room and in the passageway were red to provide night adaptation for our eyes, but on this particular morning, that made very little difference, because the night was completely black without the slightest hint of moon or star. During briefing we had been given plane assignments with deck spot, which is the relative location of the planes by number on the flight deck. With this knowledge, I proceeded upon reaching the flight deck to feel my way forward, plane by plane, until I reached my assigned number 14. We were all particularly careful at this time about our movements on the flight deck at night because of our earlier loss of the plane captain. I climbed into my F6F and, with the plane captain's help, went through the routine, attaching my harness to the seat pack that contained both parachute and life raft, fastening the shoulder straps and seat belt, plugging in my headset, and plugging in and stowing the oxygen mask.

When the bull horn sounded the "Prepare to start engines," I primed the Pratt & Whitney. This was followed by "Start engines," so I hit the switch that fired the cartridge starter. The 2,000-horsepower powerplant kicked and caught. I use this description because the cartridge was fired in a chamber much like a shotgun. The cartridge itself contained only powder that was ignited electrically by passage of a current through a high-resistance element. Instead of shot, the cartridge fired against a piston whose movement was geared to turn the engine. If no cylinder fired, the impulse was usually insufficient to produce more than one or two revolutions. However, if even one cylinder fired, the additional impulse from that cylinder was normally adequate to cause the other cylinders to initiate their firing sequence. Thus the terminology "kicked and fired" is quite accurate. In Hellcats that I flew in the postwar Naval Reserve, these cartridge starters were replaced with direct-drive electric starters.

After the start, a preflight check of the aircraft was made, consisting of checking the pressure and temperature gauges, setting the fuel selector on the right tank, setting the trim tabs, and checking the oxygen, controls, and hydraulic and electrical systems. The final check was of the engine — cycling the prop to be sure the rpm governor was functioning and checking both magnetos to be sure both ignition systems were working properly. The ignition check involved an initial movement of the mixture control from automatic lean to automatic rich because, during normal operation on deck, the engine was run at low rpm in lean to keep the plugs from fouling. The propeller control was placed into full high pitch to minimize rpm, the throttle was advanced to increase the manifold pressure, and the magnetos were checked when the manifold pressure was sufficiently high. This contrasts with the low pitch and high rpm that is used for checking magnetos when ashore. The reason for using high pitch on the carrier was the tight packing of aircraft and personnel on the flight deck. The use of high pitch minimized the induced propwash and the attendant possibility of anything astern, particularly man or aircraft, from being blown overboard. Because we were operating under blackout conditions, this was all done solely with the dim fluorescent illumination from the instrument dials.

On this particular night my aircraft was in the number one spot, so I was the first to be launched. When the air officer gave the command to launch aircraft, the taxi director lit his wands. I locked my brakes because he almost immediately gave the signal to the plane handlers to remove the chocks. He then taxied me forward about a fuselage length and gave the signal to spread the wings, at which time I moved the hydraulic selector to wing lock. With the selector in this position the system was pressurized so that movement of either wing to its extended position by the deck crew activated a valve that moved a locking pin into place. After both wings were extended, I pulled another handle to drop the "beer cans." This operation safetied the locking pins so that they could not be inadvertently withdrawn. The "beer cans" were red cylindrical-shaped indicators, one on either wing root, and their name was a result of their size and shape. When dropped, their tops were flush with the wings and a locking device was activated to prevent inadvertent wing folding.

The taxi director then taxied me onto the catapult. There the tail was attached to a hold-back and the bridle was attached to the landing gear. The catapult shoe was brought forward to tension the bridle and plane against the hold-back, and I checked to be sure that my flaps were in the full down position. The catapult officer's wand gave a rotating windup signal, and I advanced the throttle to full open. After checking the tachometer and manifold pressure gauges to be sure I was getting full power, I flipped the switch to turn on the running lights, which was the signal to launch; during daylight this would have been replaced by a salute.

I immediately locked my left hand around the throttle to prevent it from retarding during the launch. I also put my right hand on the stick and braced it with my elbow against my stomach to prevent a pitch-up and stall immediately after takeoff. In addition, I braced my head against the headrest and my back against the rear of the seat, and I had earlier checked the security of my plotting board under the instrument panel. There were known instances where improper stowage of these plotting boards allowed them to fly back during catapult shots to give a careless pilot a nasty impact in the general vicinity of his Adam's apple. When my running lights came on, the catapult officer monitored the pitching motion of the carrier. As the bow started to rise, he swung his body forward and down with both wands pointing forward, signaling the man at the catapult control to fire the catapult. Almost immediately something slammed against my backside and I was flying.

After being launched, I turned right 45 degrees toward our assigned rendezvous sector, retracted my wheels, and adjusted power settings. I then milked up my flaps and initiated a very gentle climb. Corky, my wingman, was airborne within 90 seconds. I was just reaching our rendezvous sector when he joined on my wing at which time I turned my running lights to dim to ease the strain on his eyes. We had completed only a little over a quarter of an orbiting turn when we went into the clouds. I used the VHF radio to inform the remainder of the flight of the low ceiling, and, with ten more planes pouring into the rendezvous area, I didn't even consider letting down out of the cloud. Instead, I set a course for Morotai and initiated a normal climb.

Morotai lay roughly 100 miles ahead; if we missed it, the next land on this heading was Borneo, another 700 to 800 miles across the Celebes Sea. We climbed steadily to above 20,000 feet and remained in solid cloud. The lead pilot in a formation flying in cloud utilizes his instruments to control the attitude and speed of the formation. Wingmen, on the other hand, fly tight formations and maintain their attitude and speed by reference to their neighboring plane. When maneuvering in cloud, the fluid in your inner ear flows around, and because this is the portion of your anatomy that tells you about your balance, it is not uncommon for a pilot to become disoriented with a condition known as vertigo. With vertigo, a pilot may be flying in a smooth, straight, and level flight and yet feel he is in some wild configuration, such as a vertical bank.

Because we had not broken into the clear by climbing, we tried to escape the cloud by deviating to either side of the direct heading, but without success. Some time during this maneuvering, Corky apparently developed vertigo, because during one of my regular checks of his position, his lights were missing. It wasn't long before I heard a voice on the radio saying, "Smitty, this is Corky. I just had a hell of an experience. If I live through this, I'll see you over Morotai." I knew he was pulling my leg and could handle the situation. I also knew there was a ceiling under the clouds and that I must now be well ahead of Corky, because I had been flying straight while he was sashaying around the sky. Also, the rest of the flight had to be behind us, because they had continued to rendezvous while we had proceeded on course. I therefore initiated a let-down, turned my running lights back to bright, and informed Corky of what I was doing.

Ultimately, my wing lights ceased to produce the misty halo characteristic of cloud, so I knew I was in the clear. I entered a figure-eight pattern with the long axis of the eight transverse to the course that I had flown. It was still inky black, so I had to continue to fly on instruments, but my attention alternated between the instrument panel and the outside direction from which Corky might appear. After some minutes of this, I was in a left turn of one of the loops of the eight when I noticed a peculiar reflection from the left running light. It struck me that the cloud below must be awfully thick and heavy, because I had never before seen such a dense reflection. I decided not to dip my wing into this cloud but to climb a little higher toward the one from which I had exited. In executing this decision, I did an instrument scan and was stunned by an altimeter reading of a negative 50 feet. That peculiar reflection had been from the surface of the ocean, for I had almost flown inadvertently into the water. Fortunately, God looks after drunks and fools. I had made a mistake, and I resolved that it would not be repeated.

I continued my figure-eight at a safer height above the water, and it wasn't too long before red and green wing lights appeared from the correct direction. We had managed to find each other again over this broad expanse of water. Corky again tucked onto my wing and we continued on course below the cloud; a short time later, we came clear of the cloud cover into a gray dawn.

After arrival at Morotai, Corky and I were assigned a patrol at 10,000 feet from Pitoe on the southern tip of Morotai to Galela on the northern tip of Halmahera. Such patrolling with absolutely nothing of interest happening and with the hard rims of the tinned water rations pushing into your buttocks can become very tedious. Each time we flew over the Halmahera end of our patrol, we could see that a volcano near that location was active. It was smoking, and several streams of lava were flowing down the northern slope into the sea. After the umpteenth trip back and forth, curiosity got the best of us and we descended to mountain-top level and flew over the crater and down the mountainside. We got a good, close look at an active volcano, but while making a second pass the fighter-director station called with a vector.

We were sent south to cover a ditched TBM in case the Japs tried either by sea or air to get at the crew. This was the fourth plane lost in two days. Our climb from Galela had been at full throttle, and we arrived at Wasile Bay only a few minutes later than if we had been on station. Those few minutes would have made no difference to the ultimate result, so I have no regrets about taking a close look at a live volcano. The TBM was from one of the other carriers and a doctor from that ship had climbed aboard before takeoff to get a first-hand view of the war from the air. The pilot was wounded by the shell that brought the plane down, and the doctor was lost in an attempt to save the pilot.

The carriers were scheduled to remain on station to provide air cover for the troops on Morotai until the Army engineers could put the Pitoe airstrip on the southern extremity of the island into operational status. Once this was accomplished, Army Air Forces planes could be flown in to provide the necessary air cover. The air group had most often operated with the Marines and Seabees and were accustomed to island airstrips being made operational within three to five days. But the Army engineers took twice that long, and CarDiv 22 was not released until the tenth day after the landing, 24 September. The carriers were harassed by Jap submarines almost every night because they had to cruise in a restricted area to remain within operational air distance of the island.

During the remaining period of the stay, most flights were patrols with a limited number of strikes. One of the latter was typically uneventful and involved the strafing of aircraft on an airfield on Miti, a very small island that was located just east of and quite close to the northern peninsula of Halmahera. It soon became apparent that all of the aircraft on the ground were already unserviceable as a result of strikes by Army Air Forces planes from New Guinea. There was no Japanese response, so the effort was primarily target practice, but this did provide good close-up views of a variety of Japanese aircraft, which improved recognition skills.

One incident while operating in the Dutch East Indies brought home how fateful little things can be. In this instance, a pilot from another carrier unintentionally committed suicide by an incorrect use of his radio. A "Mayday" transmission had come through on guard channel. A "Mayday" preface to a message is a signal of an emergency with imminent danger. The pilot's message indicated that the transmitting aircraft had suffered loss of engine power and that he was descending toward a water landing. Several stations answered his call, but apparently he did not hear any of them. He simply repeated his "Mayday" call several times before he left the air. He never gave a position and neglected to consider that someone might have heard his calls, even though he did not hear an answer. If he had only given some clue as to his location, a Dumbo air-sea rescue plane or a destroyer could have been dispatched to provide some chance of a rescue. With no clue as to what portion of that gigantic sea to search, any probability of finding him was negligible. It was frustrating to hear his pleas for help terminate in a long, foreboding silence.

Chapter 10

From the Dutch East Indies to the Philippines

DEPARTURE from the Dutch East Indies was with anticipation because personnel in the air group again expected to be relieved and rotated stateside after this operation. The normal tour of duty for a Navy air group throughout the war was six to eight months. At the completion of a tour, a group would be rotated back to the U.S. to be reorganized and retrained. Air Group 60 had gone aboard ship in October 1943 and, on the basis of chronology, should have been replaced after the Marianas operation. However, because of the efficiency of the *Sangamons* in their role of close-air support, the Pacific Command had decided to extend the tour for the air group through the Morotai operation. Letters between CarDiv 22 pilots and their peers on the fast carriers showed that CarDiv 22 pilots had been flying more strikes per month than were the pilots from the fast carriers. The primary difference was that the fast carriers had access to juicy targets that were previously untouched and had the opportunity for a significant amount of air-to-air combat. In contrast, the air groups on the *Sangamon*-class carriers were tied to the vicinity of an invasion and had the chore of supporting the ground troops and interdicting the enemy planes on the ground to keep them out of the air.

On return to the Admiralties at the end of September, there was again disappointment: Air Group 60 was informed that it would participate in the invasion of the Philippines. Rear Admiral T. L. "Tommy" Sprague commanding CarDiv 22 considered the geographic location of the Philippines to be conducive to night air attacks by the enemy, such as had been experienced regularly in the Marianas. He therefore thought it desirable to have one of the carriers current in night operations. Because Air Group 60 aboard the *Suwannee* appeared to the Admiral to be the most proficient, VF 60 was elected to make any night patrols or interceptions. Night field carrier landing practice was therefore undertaken — but not just by the VF pilots. All pilots in the *Suwannee's* air group were deployed to Pitylu, though I don't know why. Four satisfactory approaches and landings were required for qualification. Because *Suwannee* aircraft had not been flown ashore, this practice was to be done with CASU aircraft on the Pitylu airstrip. Pilots were ferried ashore in landing barges. The airstrip on Pitylu, like the one at Eniwetok, extended from water's edge at one end to water's edge at the other; thus, there were no obstacles at either end. However, the runway elevation was only two to three feet above the water level. This contrasts with the flight deck of the *Suwannee*, which was about 70 feet above water level. So while a plane could safely descend several feet below optimum flight path in a carrier approach, it could not do so in a field approach to the island.

Qualifications were held on a black, moonless night with partial cloud cover. There wasn't much wind, so the landing signal officer (LSO) chose to set up his station at the west end of the runway, which was closest to the living quarters. The same signals were used at night as in the daytime, but with lighted red wands rather than brightly colored paddles. The LSO judged an approaching plane's attitude and speed from a set of focused lights of different colors in the left wing. These produced a color shift as the pitch attitude of the plane changed. Normally, four planes were in the landing pattern at the same time and were equally spaced around a racetrack geometry. Several other pilots and I were scheduled with one of the early groups and completed our four landings with no difficulty. When finished, we elected to watch the others for a while and joined a group of spectators at the end of the runway on the outboard side of the LSO. In this position we could see everything that went on without interfering with the LSO's operation. A group of fighters qualified, and they were followed by a group of TBMs. There were occasional wave-offs, the signal to abort a landing attempt and go around for another try, but generally the boys were doing a commendable job. The routine was upset by one of the TBM pilots, however. This pilot made a quite acceptable approach, and as he came into the appropriate position, the LSO gave him a cut. He thereupon chopped his throttle and proceeded to land. As he passed by the LSO, there was enough light from the wands, running lights, and exhaust stacks to tell that the wheels were still retracted into the wings. The plane completed what would have been a normal landing and slid along the ground on its belly. A jeep was immediately manned to go to the plane to assist the occupants. As the jeep's lights came on to illuminate the plane, the wheels were leaving the wings, indicating that someone had just moved the landing gear selector to the down position. He was pursuing the old Navy adage, "Even if caught red-handed, pursue a course of vigorous denial."

When the runway was cleared, landing operations resumed. I continued to watch for a bit longer but finally decided to go back to my Quonset hut to read. Since the complex of huts was only a few hundred yards from the runway, the engine noise from the aircraft in the pattern was quite audible. Alone in the hut I could hear the steady drone of each plane in its approach followed by a rapid and smooth engine deceleration when it received a cut or an additional burst of power if the plane received a wave-off. I had become used to this routine and thought it peculiar when I heard the drone of an approaching plane go to full power and then suddenly and instantly go silent. But while this was odd, there was nothing further that was unusual, so I attributed my uneasiness over what I had heard to an overactive imagination and resumed reading. Fish Fischer came into the hut 15 or 20 minutes later and said, "Smitty, was Charlie Lamb a good friend of yours?"

"Was? What do you mean, 'was'?" I responded. "He *is* a good friend of mine!"

"Not any more," was the answer. "He got low in his approach, and when his wheels hit the water it dumped him upside down on the reef. He drowned in relatively shallow water before they could get him out."

Nothing more was said — what could anyone say?

Pilots were ferried back aboard ship in late September 1944, and when the fleet was assembled, the ship got underway for the Philippines. It wasn't long before the Admiral decided to exercise his night duty carrier. The LSO had chosen 12 of 30 fighter pilots for night duty. The first four selected for the first flight of the new program were Lip Singleton, Earl "Skinhead" Helwig, Rabbi Shea, and myself. We launched before dark and were assigned to patrol at a fairly low altitude. Every time we came close to the carriers, we tucked into a tight four-plane echelon with wing-in-cockpit-type parade formation. We intended to put on a decent show for the fleet, and apparently we did, because even Butch Vincent, the skipper of the torpedo squadron, said we looked good going over the ships. The utility of the flight, however, was questionable. We landed at dusk with wands and without mishap.

It was only a short time later that the Admiral changed his mind and he decided that the *Santee* would be the night duty carrier. Why he made the change is unknown; possibly it was motivated by the earlier crash landing and resulting fire aboard the *Sangamon*, the loss of two planes during night field carrier practice, or both. Certainly the lighter and slower FM2s aboard the *Santee* could, in principle, be brought aboard with less hazard than the faster and heavier F6Fs aboard the other *Sangamons*. Although this selection of the *Santee* may have been a step in the right direction, it was soon proven that the entire concept of a night fighter without radar on board was fruitless. The proof occurred several nights later when Harold Funk, the skipper of the *Santee's* fighter squadron, was launched at night with his wingman to intercept an intruder. Ship's radar vectored them onto interception several times. On some of these vectors they passed close enough to the intruder to visually observe the enemy's hot exhaust stacks, but they were completely unable to maintain contact long enough to fire a shot. The results caused the concept to be scrubbed until radar-equipped fighters became available.

While the air group was engaged at Morotai helping to advance MacArthur's drive across the South Pacific to the west, the naval drive through the Central Pacific was also continuing to advance westward. Dual operations were possible because the steadily increasing American productivity made available greater quantities of trained men, materiel, and shipping, including CVE escort carriers. Thus, in September 1944, while Morotai was in contention, the naval drive also made another step forward with a Marine invasion of Palau. It may be noted that this Marine operation was the only amphibious assault in the Pacific from October 1942 through December 1944 in which the *Suwannee* did not contribute to the air support. The landings in the Philippines that were scheduled for late October 1944 were to mark the meeting of MacArthur's Army drive across the South Pacific and Nimitz's naval drive across the Central Pacific. The Philippine invasion was to be the biggest operation yet undertaken in the Pacific War.

En route to the Philippines, violent conditions were encountered, almost as an omen of the turmoil that that was to be encountered there. This violence was in the form of a typhoon that lasted for three or four days. As one might reasonably expect, there was no flying during the storm. Indeed, it was even dangerous to go on deck, so movement throughout the ship was mainly by internal passageways. As big as she was, the ship pitched and rolled over large angles. Many found it uncomfortable, but several were lulled to sleep in their bunks. The effect of the high seas on the crews of the destroyers and destroyer escorts in the screen must, however, have been literally hell because of the excessive roll due to the very narrow beams of those ships.

Actually, even aboard a carrier the rolling was dangerous. This was explained one morning at breakfast by one of the ship's officers. A carrier is relatively top heavy and is susceptible to capsizing if the roll is too severe. In the case of the *Suwannee*, the critical angle of roll before capsizing was computed to be 27 degrees. This officer informed his listeners that he had been on watch the previous night during a period of particularly violent rolling when the inclinometer, which measures the degree of roll, actually reached this maximum angle. He said she hung at this precarious balance point for several heart-stopping seconds, apparently trying to decide whether to right herself or go on over. Then a big wave hit her down side and upset the delicate situation to move her toward the upright position. Many pilots blithely slept through all this. What it proved is that the old saw, "What you don't know can't hurt you," is a lie.

After the storm had abated somewhat, it was safe to go up onto the deck. The waves were still mountainous. One of the destroyers in the screen had had its foremast carried away. I estimated that the height of that destroyer from the waterline to the top of the bridge was on the order of 40 feet; in comparison, when on the flight deck of the carrier, you were about 70 feet above the waterline. Yet, when both the destroyer and the carrier were down in wave troughs, the destroyer was completely hidden by an intervening wall of water. To say that the sight is impressive is a gross understatement — awesome is more appropriate. To most, this brought home the insignificance of an individual human being in comparison to the forces of nature on this minor planet in the vast universe.

It can only be imagined what went through the minds of the crew of the destroyer that had lost its mast. It was reported that the destroyer captain had contacted Admiral Sprague at the peak of the storm, when the mast had been lost, and had requested permission to come about and run for a sheltered port. The Admiral wisely refused the request, for had the captain turned out of the wind to come about, he most surely would have broached and capsized. The fact that the destroyer captain even considered such a maneuver meant that his ship was taking a terrible pounding. The Pacific Ocean is capable of extreme conditions. During the *Suwannee's* cruise, sea conditions were at the extremes, at some times completely inverse to the violent wave action of the typhoon. In one instance, water conditions were such that the water was glassy smooth with not so much as a ripple on the surface, only a gentle undulation with an amplitude of only a foot or two and a distance of more than a mile between crests.

After the days within the most violent part of the typhoon and no air reconnaissance, Admiral Sprague was becoming anxious. Air operations were therefore resumed as soon as feasible. I was scheduled as a member of the first flight, and the waves were still quite high and the ship was still pitching over large angles. The carrier was headed into the wind and was slowed to the point where the screws were making only enough turns to maintain steerage. Even so, the wind across the flight deck exceeded 50 knots. During the launch, the catapult officer was very careful to time each shot so that the bow was rising to help lift the catapulted plane into the air. After becoming airborne, the wind was steady and not particularly rough, so the flight itself was uneventful. Upon returning to the carrier, conditions had not changed, so I wondered what the landing would be like. It turned out to be the easiest carrier landing imaginable. When the wind velocity was subtracted from the F6F's 69-knot approach speed, it meant that the plane was approaching the carrier at less than 20 knots. It seemed to take all day to fly the final leg of the pattern to reach the ship. The LSO had plenty of time to choose the moment for the cut, and he timed his signal so that deck was rising to meet the landing planes rather than falling away.

While proceeding toward the Philippines, there was a briefing as to the nature of the impending operation. It was to be the biggest amphibious operation yet undertaken in the Pacific and was to involve a joint Army and Marine landing on the island of Leyte, which lies between the islands of Samar and Mindanao on the eastern side of the Philippine group. The three islands surround the body of water known as Leyte Gulf. The briefers stated that, for the most part, U.S. aviators could expect friendly treatment from the native population if they were forced down in the Philippines. An exception might be on the southern island of Mindanao, where the majority of the natives were Mohammedan; their views concerning Americans were varied, and we were warned to exercise care should we be forced down there. We were also told that should we encounter a friendly Mindanaon who offered food and shelter, it would be wise to accept graciously, no matter how unappetizing. Further, if he offered one of the family females to share the night, it would be prudent to at least take her into our sleeping quarters, even if nothing else was done. To refuse such an offer would be a gross insult to the host and would probably be worth the guest's life.

The *Suwannee* was to be part of a fleet of 18 CVEs to be stationed in three divisions of six each. The ships were to operate approximately 100 miles east of Leyte over the Philippine trench, whose deepest point is near 5,700 fathoms, slightly deeper than the deepest part of the Mariana trench. The 18 carriers were to form carrier Task Group 77.4; Rear Admiral Tommy Sprague aboard the *Sangamon* was in overall command of the Task Group in addition to the southernmost division of six carriers. This southernmost Carrier Group 77.4.1 was code-designated as Taffy 1 and consisted of the four *Sangamons* plus two Kaiser-built carriers, the *Petrof Bay* and the *Saginaw Bay*. The six carriers that were to form the central Carrier Group 77.4.2 were designated Taffy 2 with Rear Admiral F. B. Stump commanding. The six northernmost carriers were to be Carrier Group 77.4.3, designated Taffy 3, with Rear Admiral C. A. F. "Ziggy" Sprague commanding.

Troops were to go ashore at Leyte on 20 October 1944, but other activities were to begin earlier. In particular, flight operations were to begin predawn on the 18th, and shortly after air cover became available, the "char ladies" (minesweepers) were to clear Leyte Gulf for entry by the invasion fleet. The fleet was to consist of battleships, cruisers, and destroyers for both shore bombardment and for protection against Japanese naval units, troop transports to bring the invasion force, and supply ships to carry the wide variety of materiel required by an invasion force. The weather continued to abate, and arrival off the Philippines was in time to begin operations as scheduled. My first operational flight in the Philippines turned out to be the longest flight that I ever made in a single-engine aircraft.

Chapter 11

The Philippines: Initial Phase, 18-24 October 1944

IN the early hours of 18 October, CarDiv 22 was on station over the Philippine Deep around 100 to 150 miles east of Leyte, and Fish Fischer's division — consisting of Fish, Mac McManemin, Corky Finley, and me — was briefed to be part of a "group grope" that was to involve planes from several air groups from the carrier division. Launch was to be pre-dawn followed by a strike against the Japanese-held airfields on northern Negros. To get to Negros, we had to fly west across Leyte, the Camotes Sea, and northern Cebu. The dawn was still only gray as we passed over the Camotes Sea, and it was evident that there was heavy cloud buildup in the west. By the time we reached Cebu, we found it expedient to divert north around the tip of the island. After passage of this northern tip, the cloud development became progressively heavier, and as we continued, it soon became obvious that the heavy cover would make it impossible to find any targets on Negros. The flight was, therefore, shifted to an alternate target — an airfield called Opon on a small island just big enough to accommodate the field. This island was located just offshore about halfway down the east coast of Cebu.

The attack group worked over that airfield pretty well and the men were confident that they left most, if not all, of the visible Japanese aircraft in non-operational status. Enemy ground fire was fairly intense but was mostly of light caliber. One of the group's F6Fs started streaming a trail of smoke from what looked like his belly tank as he passed over the airfield. It was later determined that the stricken plane was off the *Sangamon* and that it was flown by a fellow who had gone through training with me and Dew Timm. Someone called him on the radio and told him of his problem. He acted quickly and decisively. He was headed northeast toward the Camotes Sea, and as he passed the field boundary he pulled into a climb and continued seaward. At what looked to be about 300 feet while still climbing, he opened his canopy, half-rolled the airplane, unbuckled his safety belt, and fell free of the aircraft. His parachute barely had time to fully blossom before he hit water. His plane, without guidance, dropped its nose to plunge vertically into the sea. The pilot was something under a mile offshore from both the airfield and the island of Cebu. He soon was free of his parachute and had his rubber raft inflated.

In the meantime, the flight leaders were holding a radio consultation. Obviously, if the pilot were left on his own, the Japanese would soon be out to pick him up. It was therefore decided that Fish's division should remain to fly cover over him while attempting to get an air-sea rescue plane to pick him up. Selection of an F6F Hellcat division rather than an FM2 Wildcat division to remain was logical, because the F6Fs had significantly greater endurance than the FM2s. With the departure of the other planes in the attack group, Fish and Mac climbed to 20,000 feet in order to establish contact with air-sea rescue via the line-of-sight VHF radio, and Corky climbed to patrol at 10,000 feet. I remained to patrol at 5,000 feet, but I first made a low pass near to the downed pilot. He waved to let me know that he was all right.

After some time, a native canoe put out from the Cebu shore and paddled toward him. I made a pass over the canoe to assure myself that it was a Filipino and not a Jap; I then returned to my station. The canoe continued to the life raft, and the *Sangamon* pilot climbed from one into the other. He deflated his life raft and took it aboard the canoe. Just as they were starting back to the shore, I saw a Japanese aircraft initiating a run on the small craft. I immediately peeled into a dive, simultaneously hit both gun chargers, and turned on the arming switches and gunsight. The Jap pilot must have seen me shortly after I entered the dive, because he almost immediately changed course and high-tailed it for the island. I bent the throttle against the stop and followed. The Jap plane was what was called an Oscar and was the first-line fighter of the Japanese army (the Zeke was the first-line fighter of their navy). I wanted to get close before opening fire because I wanted to be sure of getting hits. The Oscar grew larger in my gun sight as the distance between us shrank.

Just as I was ready to fire, the Jap disappeared into the cloud cover over Cebu. Our planes were going so fast that I couldn't help but follow into the cloud. However, I immediately executed a chandelle — a steep climbing turn to the left or right resulting in a 180-degree reversal in direction — to change course, because there is a spine of mountains running north and south near the east coast of the island and our planes were at a very low altitude. I was very frustrated; I really wanted a piece of that Jap. I should have gambled and loosed a burst or two at longer range with at least a chance, albeit a lesser chance, of getting some vital hits. Nobody could have been any more critical of my error than I was. The next time would be different.

By then, the division had been in the air over five hours and still had a flight of approximately 200 miles to make. No air-sea rescue plane had yet been dispatched to the downed *Sangamon* pilot. The four planes of Fish's division rendezvoused and continued to orbit until the pilot and his guide had paddled almost to the shore. The story of how he was treated by the Filipinos and was hidden from the Japs until he could be returned to our forces was published in *Life* magazine in 1945. It was later rumored that he was paid $10,000 for his story. After the canoe reached shore, it was felt that we had done everything that could be done, and our four-man division departed for the ship. We each checked our fuel supply. Though it looked as if everyone had a safe amount, no one considered that he had a huge surplus, so we did what we could to conserve fuel during the trip home. All belly tanks in the flight were empty, and so were my left main tank and reserve tank. Corky and I, and probably Fish and Mac, went to full high pitch which, with the manifold pressure that was being used, gave between 1,100 and 1,200 rpm. We also went to manual lean and weaned the fuel-air mixture until it was just above the point of spontaneous detonation. The engines were practically running on fumes. Because these engines were geared down to drive the propeller at a ratio of 16 to 9, you could almost count the blades as they turned. How far out the ship was from the islands on that particular day is unknown, but that flight seemed to last an inordinately long time.

We finally reached the carriers, which were aware of our fuel status; they soon turned into the wind to take us aboard without a prolonged hold. The elapsed time for the flight was six hours and 35 minutes. My fuel gauge showed that I still had 70 gallons in the right main tank. At the rate that I was burning fuel on the last leg of the flight, that would have been enough for another hour to hour and a half, but it would not have left much in reserve for a carrier approach. It was estimated that each carrier approach consumed 15 to 20 gallons.

This was only the beginning of our Philippine phase of the war, and in the productive period of 18 through 24 October, the air group was kept very busy attacking a variety of targets in the air, on the ground, and on the water — mostly targets of opportunity. Early strikes over the Visayans, located between Luzon and Mindanao, garnered Lip Singleton a small transport; Fish, Mac, and Corky some PT boats; and Luke MacKay and Bugs Beidelman, both of VT, a pair of small freighters. Over this period, Mac and Willie Schmall shared credit for downing first a Val, a Japanese single-engine dive bomber of the type that had attacked Pearl Harbor, and later a Tony, a fighter patterned after the German Me109. Mac also received full credit for scratching another Val. The first Val is believed to be VF 60's first aircraft score in the Philippines. Monty Montgomery added two more planes to his score, both Zekes.

The most impressive of VF 60's aerial combats was by Lip's division, consisting of Lip, Ralph "Kal" Kalal, Eggbert Barber, and Tex Garner. While supporting troop landings on the 20th, eight Japanese Lilys, light twin-engine bombers, came in to attack the invasion force. The division dove on the Japs and opened fire. They continued firing until they reached the anchored fleet. By then there were no more Japs — they had splashed all eight. That same day, their fuel reserves ran so low that they diverted to the nearest available carrier, which happened to be the *Franklin*, one of the big *Essex*-class carriers of Task Force 38. When they came back to the *Suwannee* they told of landing on a deck the size of the King ranch, where they taxied for what seemed like miles after landing just to get across the barriers.

The Taffy 1 carriers also saw enemy action during this time. On 20 October, four low-flying Japanese fighters approached Taffy 1, and three attacked. The fourth broke off but was intercepted and destroyed by a CAP from Taffy 2. There were nine casualties on the ships, with the *Santee* suffering minor damage from bombing and strafing and the *Sangamon* even less damage from a ricocheting bomb hit. All three Japanese planes were downed, two by the CAP and one by ships' antiaircraft fire.

In the air, carrier planes were frequently cleared to seek targets of opportunity with the primary purpose being interdiction. Minimizing the supplies to the Japanese frontline forces on Leyte was intended to minimize their effectiveness. In this work, Air Group 60 efficiently destroyed an appreciable amount of materiel useful to the Japanese. This included a large number of trucks and several small surface craft engaged in supply efforts. Unfortunately, during this time Skin Helwig was lost while on a strike on Alicante airfield on the northwest coast of Negros. He was hit and set afire while making a low pass. He tried to bail out at around 300 feet, which was insufficient for his chute to fully blossom.

The schedule was heavy with flights every day, generally for periods of four to five hours and including CAPs and troop support as well as the interdiction flights. On some of these flights, pilots were given printed sheets advertising to the Filipinos that General MacArthur was returning. Pilots were supposed to throw out the sheets to let them flutter down gently onto the landscape. But some of the pilots, who did not care for the General, just couldn't hang onto those papers longer than it took to be out of sight of the carrier and allowed their flyers to blow away into the ocean. One can only suppose that those propaganda leaflets were somehow defective. During this period of operations, losses, in addition to Skin, included two other F6Fs to operational accidents, but both pilots were recovered. On at least one occasion, the mission kept a flight airborne late enough that it was necessary to make night carrier landings. My 100th carrier landing turned out to be one of these night landings.

Although the purposes of all flights were serious, there were sometimes lighter moments. One such flight was a target CAP when 12 F6Fs were launched with orders to report to a fighter director station aboard a destroyer near the western mouth of Surigao Strait, which runs between Leyte and Dinagat at the southeastern end of Leyte. The fighter director station's call sign was Pepsi Cola and the flight's call sign for patrol missions was Joker, though for strike and interdiction missions it was Quaker. This was a time when, back in the States, there was already a battle among Pepsi Cola, Coca Cola, and Royal Crown Cola for the lion's share of the soft drink business. Pepsi and Royal Crown both came in 12-ounce bottles, while Coke came in the 8-ounce size. Pepsi had an advertising jingle then on the radio that went:

> Pepsi Cola hits the spot,
> Twelve full ounces, that's a lot.
> Far better than the other two,
> Pepsi Cola is the drink for you!

As the flight proceeded from the ship toward station, Corky called Fish, who was leading the flight, and asked permission to make the arrival report when they came on station. The request was readily granted, and in due time, Corky gave forth with:

> Pepsi Cola, we're on the spot,
> Twelve F6s, that's a lot.
> Far better than the FM2,
> Joker three is the team for you!

Everybody, including the destroyer controllers, got a chuckle out of the paraphrasing.

Routine patrols could also be exciting. Lieutenant Commander Harold Funk, skipper of the fighter squadron on the *Santee*, became an ace in one day by shooting down six Japanese planes on such a patrol. These patrols could also on occasion have some interesting moments in terms of impressive sights. In addition to the aviator's halo and the live volcano on Halmahera, another spectacular sight was found while patrolling over the western portion of Leyte: the remnant crater of a small, extinct volcano. It had filled with water to form a crater lake. From this lake ran a small stream that created a chain of three waterfalls as it flowed down the small mountain toward the sea. From the air it was quite impressive.

Interdiction flights were more likely to stimulate the adrenaline and much less prone to generate boredom than the repetition of the preset path of a patrol. During interdiction missions, pilots were almost always allowed to search for targets of opportunity. They sought powered surface craft capable of carrying reasonable-size loads from one island to another and considered these fair game. They had no intention of harming the native population. Thus small, unpowered fishing craft were left strictly alone. On one flight a vessel was caught near the center of the Camotes Sea headed in the direction of Leyte. Fishing in such deep water seemed quite unlikely, and the heading toward Leyte was inconsistent with Filipino ownership. The craft was therefore left a drifting hulk with no remaining sign of life on board.

On another occasion, the searching was along the western shore of Samar for craft capable of aiding the garrison on Leyte. The flight came across a 30- to 40-foot-long power boat in a small anchorage. There was no indication that anyone was aboard, but it was quite definitely capable of reaching Leyte with a useful load. A strafing pattern was set up and the boat was set afire so there was certainty that it was not going to help the Leyte garrison.

The belief that the flights were interdicting Japanese resupply and reinforcement of their Leyte garrison was the only justification for such destruction of useful equipment. Admittedly, there was always a possibility that one of the targets was owned by a Filipino, but under martial law it could always be commandeered and used against American (and thereby Filipino) interests. It was only hoped that the efforts were contributing to the saving of American lives.

Some interdiction flights were a bit more nerve-shattering than others. One such flight that I was involved in was over Leyte itself after the troops had gone ashore on 20 October at both Dulag and Tacloban. Our flight of four was looking for targets behind the Japanese lines, well in advance of our forces' inward expansion from their landing sites. Near Dulag, we were following one of the better roads that crossed the island when we came to a small Filipino village. The road went straight through the middle of this village; there were only a dozen or so buildings, mostly dwellings, on either side of the road. Two large Japanese trucks were parked on this road, and though they were straightbed trucks, they were nearly as large as tractor-trailer rigs. The Japanese apparently ran them at night and parked them during the day. The logic in parking them in the middle of a village seemed to be that the Japs thought Americans would leave the trucks alone rather than endanger the native population. However, the Japanese purpose was frustrated because the flight set up a strafing pattern parallel to the road so that no villagers would be hit, nor would any of their dwellings. The pattern was racetrack in form and consisted of one plane in its strafing run, the one ahead recovering from its run, the third plane moving back at altitude toward entry position, and the fourth plane ready to enter its dive when the strafing plane cleared. It wasn't long before one of the trucks was on fire. The second truck was more recalcitrant, so strafing continued.

I was surprised to note that the natives had lined up on either side of the road to watch the show, oblivious of the chance of a ricochet. Finally, I could see my tracers going into the last truck's gas tank, so I figured one more burst would do it. Sure enough, another short burst elicited a tendril of smoke, but I had forgotten how low I was getting. I noted my rapid descent and proximity to the ground and came back too rapidly on the stick. There was an instantaneous secondary stall. It lasted only a fraction of a second, but that was enough to put me close enough to the ground that, had the wheels been down, they would have been rolling. Obviously, I had some help from ground effect, additional lift produced when a plane flies very low, and there may also have been some help from above in heaven. Ahead, the road curved to the right and immediately in front was a wall of trees. However, the plane was going so fast that, when the wings took hold, the plane lifted out of there like an arrow from a bow. I had just proven that fools do repeat errors and that the lesson at Agana and the coconut grove had not sunk in deeply enough.

Another episode associated with interdiction missions occurred near a small island called Biliran that lies immediately north of Leyte. Fish's division was operating as a four-plane flight. We had split into two two-plane sections with Corky and I proceeding southward down the east side of Biliran and Fish and Mac proceeding southward down the west side of the island. Corky and I were moving rapidly, low on the water, 100 or so yards offshore; we had seen nothing of interest. I noted a native village ahead at the edge of the water, but there was obviously nothing significant there. However, the natives must have thought that they were going to be strafed, because the sound of the engines caused them to issue forth from that village into the water with the same alacrity displayed by crows flocking from their roost at the sound of a gunshot. The natives were in error. I simply rocked my wings during passage in what I hoped was a sign of friendship.

Corky and I had proceeded only a short distance farther south when a call came from Fish that he and Mac were attacking a small coaster — a vessel engaged in coastal trade — making for Leyte. We peeled up and over the island to join them. By the time we got there, we saw smoke coming from something burning just aft of the coaster's mainmast. The crew had just beached the vessel, which was about 80 to 100 feet in length with a relatively broad beam. The crew was in the process of departing the vessel by going over the side into the shallow water and scurrying into the trees beyond the sand beach. We thought that their haste was due to the machine-gun fire from the aircraft, but it shortly became plain that the motivation was even stronger. Corky and I joined the other two planes to set up a standard four-plane racetrack strafing pattern to work over the boat. We managed to encourage the smoldering fire somewhat but seemed not to be accomplishing much more until a point was reached when Fish was in his firing run, Mac was getting ready to start a dive, I had completed my recovery and was proceeding back abeam the vessel at altitude, and Corky was in the process of recovery.

It was then that the beached craft exploded. It had apparently been full of munitions. I saw rather than heard the explosion; there was actually a visible shock wave that expanded spherically from the ship. When that wave front hit the strafing plane, it appeared for an instant to be displaced backward before continuing through its dive. That impression may have been an optical illusion, but it certainly appeared that way. Later, when flying down along the beach, not a single piece of that coaster could be seen that couldn't have been picked up with a scoop shovel. When the division got back aboard the *Suwannee* over two hours later, Fish still had a deathly greenish pallor as a result of his close encounter with the man with the scythe.

It is impossible to recount all of the individual exploits that occurred during the short period of 18 to 24 October, because details have been lost with the passage of time. By the 24th, Monty Montgomery had added two more Zekes to his victory belt for a total of three. Mac McManemin had taken his second cruise in a life raft off Negros and had been picked up by the USS *Kidd*, the same destroyer that had earlier rescued Frog La Fargue. On the single day of 24 October, the air group reported shooting down nine Lilys and one Zeke. The VT crews were also busy; they flew close-air support, interdiction missions, and carried air controllers. This meant they were on the receiving end of their share of enemy fire. An example is an encounter that pitted Charley Leonard and Gene Sabin with their crews against a group of medium and heavy antiaircraft batteries. In spite of the heavy enemy fire, they got at least one direct hit on one battery. In aerial encounters, the VT crews were frustrated by the TBM's slow speed. For instance, Tim Casey vainly chased a Zeke intruder away from CarDiv 22 and lost him because of the Zeke's superior speed.

The *Suwannee's* operational station was the 100- to 150-mile area generally east of Leyte, and the next two days — 25 and 26 October — would be the period decreed by the fates for the convergence of the *Suwannee*, Air Group 60, and the kamikaze corps over the Philippine Deep.

Chapter 12

First Hole in the Flight Deck, 25 October 1944

IN the ready room on the evening of 24 October, Combat Information Center (CIC) began to feed back reports from pickets, primarily submarines. These reports came from a variety of distances and directions, but all indicated that Japanese naval units from the northeast, north, and southwest were on the move and were steaming to converge somewhere in the vicinity of Leyte Gulf. It didn't take a genius to figure that the island-hopping campaign had pushed the Japanese far enough toward their home islands that they had either to sue for peace or fight. Their ship movements indicated that they had chosen the latter.

The battle that developed has become known as the Battle of Leyte Gulf, and naval experts have deemed it one of the great naval battles in history, possibly the greatest. Certainly more ships and men were involved than in any other prior battle. There were many separate actions, so that any individual participant could have firsthand knowledge of only a small part of the whole. For reasons that will soon become obvious, participation by the *Suwannee* and her Air Group 60 lasted for only a limited time, but we contributed effectively in downing several enemy aircraft and in damaging several units of the large multicomponent Japanese naval forces. The battle began on 25 October 1944 and marks the first use by the Japanese of organized kamikaze squadrons.

History now indicates that the Japanese aimed four naval fleets at the Philippines to converge there to attack the American invasion fleet (see works by Hoyt, MacIntyre, and Koenig). Two of these fleets sortied from North Borneo. The larger and more important of the two consisted of 5 battleships, 10 heavy cruisers, 2 light cruisers, and 15 destroyers. It was intended to pass through San Bernardino Strait north of Samar, sail south, and attack the U.S. invasion fleet in Leyte Gulf from the northeast. This large Japanese fleet included the battleship *Yamato* with 18-inch naval rifles, the biggest in the world, and was commanded by Admiral Kurita. The second fleet from Borneo consisted of two battleships, a heavy cruiser, a light cruiser, and four destroyers and was commanded by Admiral Nishimura. It was intended to pass south of Leyte and through Surigao Strait to attack the invasion fleet from the south. A third fleet under Admiral Shima sortied from the Inland Sea on the west side of the Japanese home islands with the mission of supporting and cooperating with Nishimura. This fleet consisted of two heavy cruisers, one light cruiser, and four destroyers. The fourth and last fleet also sortied from the Inland Sea. It was under the command of Admiral Ozawa and consisted of one heavy carrier, three light carriers, two battleships, three light cruisers, and eight destroyers. Ozawa's four carriers had only 116 planes among them, far less than their full complement of aircraft. However, their mission was not to engage the American fleet in a decisive battle but rather to serve as a decoy to lure the U.S. fleet of fast carriers, Task Force 38, far enough to the northeast to leave the invasion fleet without air cover. In this endeavor, the Japanese were partially successful, because Admiral Halsey, commander of the American fast carrier fleet, did take this bait and pursued Ozawa to the northeast. However, the ruse cost the Japanese all four carriers. Furthermore, the Japanese plan to strip the invasion fleet of air cover didn't take into consideration the 18 American CVEs.

These details were, of course, unknown on the morning of 25 October. I was part of the first flight that was scheduled for a pre-dawn takeoff from the *Suwannee*; our four planes were to fly combat air patrol over southern Leyte. During the early morning briefing, pilots were informed that some night fighting between surface units had already occurred as a Japanese fleet had tried to penetrate through to the invasion fleet via Surigao Strait. The Shima and Nishimura fleets had arrived. At that preflight briefing, there was still no word as to the outcome of the fighting in Surigao Strait, but a torpedo strike from the *Suwannee* was in preparation before our CAP was launched. The day promised a lot of action, and pilots were anxious to go.

As aircraft were manned and pilots performed their preflight checks, I found a malfunction in my assigned plane and, therefore, climbed out and went to the standby plane and displaced the standby pilot. On any flight where less than the ship's full complement of aircraft was scheduled, an additional reserve or standby aircraft was manned and was included on the schedule. This plane was launched only if one of the others aborted the flight. More than once a standby pilot was launched when he had not expected to fly — on one occasion, at least, for a five-hour flight on an empty stomach. On this morning, one of the other pilots in the flight also found a malfunction, so even with the standby aircraft, only three planes were launched.

It was still very dark as Monty Montgomery, Dew Timm, and I proceeded to the island. We were scheduled to patrol at 20,000 feet back and forth over southern Leyte from Surigao Strait to Ormoc Bay. We arrived as dawn was breaking and reported to the control station. He had had no radar contacts, so we took up the patrol. We continued to bore a hole in the air, plodding back and forth, and were held on station beyond the scheduled time without being told why our relief would be late. At that time we did not know that all aircraft not otherwise assigned were engaged against Kurita's force, which had penetrated through San Bernardino Strait and attacked Taffy 3 off Samar. On patrol, all we knew was that our fuel supply was being diminished.

At the northern extremity of the patrol at Ormoc Bay, we had encountered a flight of four FM2s that were patrolling the area. It was, therefore, no surprise when, as we three neared Ormoc Bay at 20,000 feet during one cycle of the extended patrol, we noted a flight of four aircraft approaching from the northeast. However, as they got closer, I was surprised to spot a fifth aircraft gently S-turning about 500 feet below and almost directly under the other flight. It was a Zeke! I called a "Tally ho" on the radio, dropped my belly tank, and charged my guns. Monty and Dew must have seen the Zeke at about the same time, because we all initiated a dive together. Once committed, I wondered why the FM2s did not recognize that our F6Fs were onto something and follow to see what it was. I glanced over to see what the other flight was doing and was dumbfounded to note that, instead of the flight of four FM2s that I had tacitly assumed them to be, we were preparing to dive under a flight of four Zekes. We had taken the sucker bait. I immediately altered course to come around onto the tails of the upper four Zekes and called a radio warning to my shipmates. They, too, altered course to get a shot at the higher group. When the Japs saw what was happening, their formation broke apart like a clay pigeon impacted by shotgun pellets.

We each picked a Zeke to follow. My target descended in a diving right-hand turn. A Zeke at high speed rolls relatively easily from right to left but has a tough time rolling left to right. The root of this roll behavior is that the Zero was designed without an aileron trim tab. But in this right-hand diving turn, G-forces were too high on both of us for accurate firing. Furthermore, I found that as we rapidly descended into warmer air, the cold cockpit canopy condensed moisture to obscure my vision. I turned on the defroster, but until it warmed sufficiently, I had to rub the windows vigorously and often to keep from being completely blind. Highly restricted visibility when bullets are apt to fly is a rather less than comfortable situation. The Jap continued his spiraling descent until we got so low that he had to give it up. He then headed out over Ormoc Bay toward the Camotes Sea. Once he straightened out, I got off a good burst. I could see the tracers and incendiaries hitting him, but I didn't strike anything vital, so I tried again but with the same result. We were both flying at full throttle, but the F6F is faster than the Zeke, so I was getting closer all the time.

At the instant I pressed the trigger to fire the next burst, he dumped both his landing gear and flaps. It was like slamming on the brakes. To miss ramming him I had to execute a steep chandelle to the left and immediately follow this with a diving turn also to the left to come back to my original heading astern of the Jap plane. The diving turn brought my speed back to near what it had been, and the maneuver amounted to a 360-degree turn in a steeply inclined angle. Since the Jap had slowed significantly by his maneuver, he was now re-accelerating, but I rapidly overtook him. He again tried the same move, but I was ready for him and put a burst into his right wing root where the gas tank was located. The incendiaries ignited the gasoline, and he blew apart. I must say that it gave a strange feeling to fly through the debris of an exploding airplane. The pieces rained down onto the water, and by the time I had completed another 360-degree turn, there was no longer any evidence that there had ever been another aircraft in the vicinity. I found out later that each of the three of us had gotten the Jap that he chased. Monty's was number four for him. We regretted that the scattering of their formation had allowed two of them to get away. In any case, I felt that I had

A rare photograph of a Japanese Zero. The aircraft was on display at an airfield in China after being captured in February 1943.

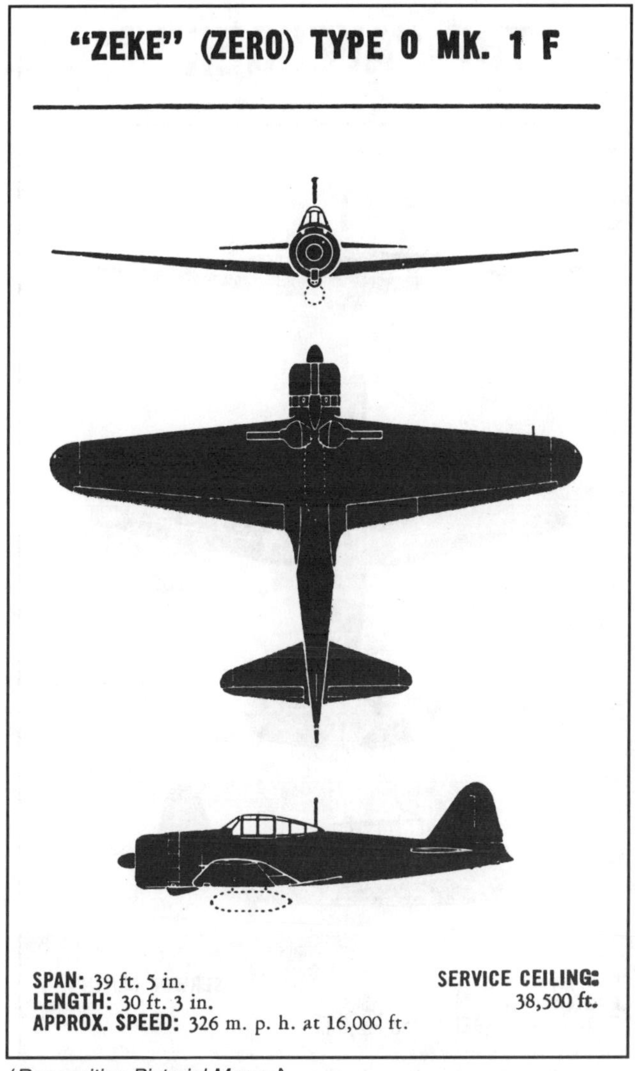

(*Recognition Pictorial Manual*)

lost my "virginity" and had done for the first time what a fighter pilot is trained to do.

I then headed back toward Ormoc Bay. I established radio contact with Dew, but Monty was apparently out of range. I told Dew that my engine had overheated during the full-throttle chase and that it was running rough with

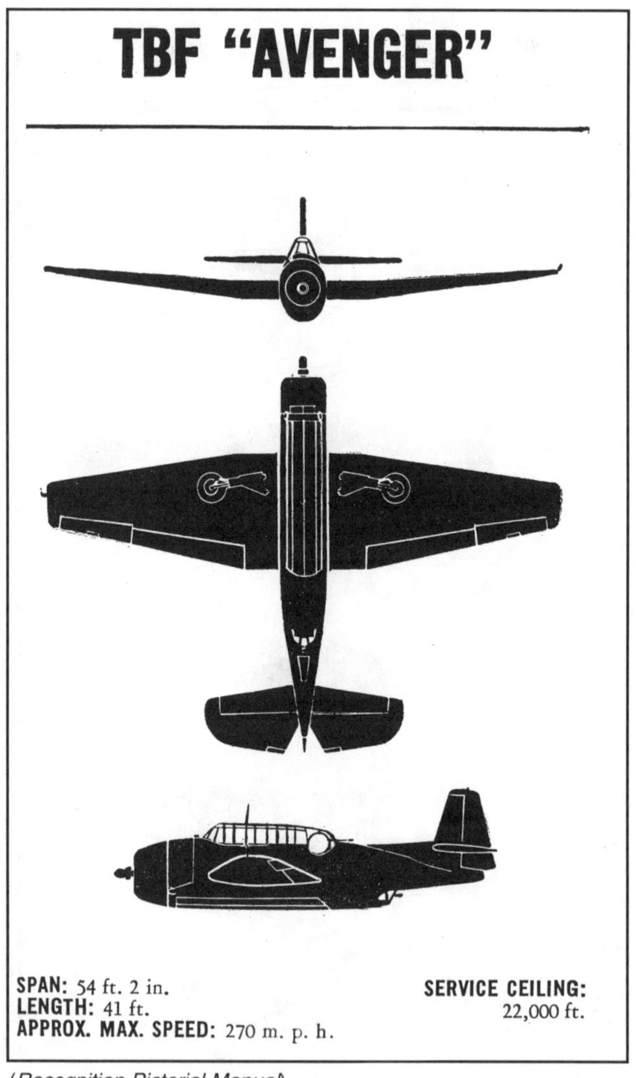

(*Recognition Pictorial Manual*)

occasional detonation but that I was heading to rendezvous with him over a little islet located in Ormoc Bay. We soon met up, and because of our low fuel status we elected to go to the captured airstrip at Tacloban rather than attempt a flight to the ship. We flew across Leyte and then northward, just inland of the east shore. We chose this route to avoid flying over the invasion fleet that was anchored offshore, because our past experience led us to believe that they would shoot first and ask questions later. When we arrived at Tacloban, we found that we were not unique. Carrier aircraft were flocking in like migrating waterfowl into a pond.

Over 100 aircraft were either in the landing pattern or already on the ground. Upon landing, we found the earth to be soft and sandy because of the recent rain, and considerable throttle with full back stick was required to keep from nosing over during the roll-out. It was quite evident that, if the Japanese were using this field regularly, their aircraft must have been considerably lighter than the U.S. planes. Several of the landing planes went over on their backs, including VF 60's own skipper.

The ground crew of an Army Air Forces squadron had already come ashore, and their supplies were beginning to build up. The Navy aircraft were able to get fuel and ammunition from this detachment. Monty also landed at Tacloban, but something was wrong with his airplane. He and the skipper were stuck ashore and had to find surface transportation before ultimately rejoining the squadron later after the ship's return to Sea Adler Harbor.

While at Tacloban, the airfield underwent a Japanese dive-bombing attack. The Japs may have hit something, but as far as one could tell, no airplanes on the flight line or anything of importance received damage. It was learned that most of the planes at Tacloban were from Taffy 3, the northernmost group of carriers. It seems that these planes had been launched when their carrier division had come under Kurita's attack at 0649, following initial contact at 0645. The planes expended what ordnance they had aboard and then headed for the beach, some for Tacloban and some for Dulag. At this time there was very little information, but it is now known that Kurita's force had slipped through San Bernardino Strait unnoticed after Halsey's fleet had been lured north by Ozawa. In retrospect, Kurita's handling of his fleet is confusing. He was apparently surprised to find carriers that far north, because a Japanese plane had earlier reported sighting carriers much farther south. It would thus appear that the reporting plane had sighted Taffy 1. It is believed that Kurita mistook the CVEs for fast fleet carriers.

In the early hours of 25 October 1944, the *Suwannee* had received word about the battle in progress in Surigao Strait. As a result, four torpedo planes were armed with torpedoes. Butch Vincent and three other VT pilots — Bugs Beidelman, Luke MacKay, and Frank Langdon — plus two VT from the *Sangamon* were launched pre-dawn with the aim of finding the Japanese ships in or near Surigao Strait. Escorting fighters were sent for protection and carried bombs. They found the Japanese retreating from the strait after already losing a number of ships to Task Group 77.2, which consisted of 8 old battleships, 9 cruisers, and 22 destroyers and was under the command of Admiral Oldendorf. The Japanese had also been harassed by motor torpedo boat squadrons that deployed in the Surigao approaches. Nishimura and Shima were outnumbered and outgunned.

Worse still from the Japanese standpoint was that penetration of Surigao Strait by Nishimura's and Shima's groups was not coordinated. Nishimura had penetrated first. The surface battle began shortly after 0300 on 25 October. By 0430, Nishimura had lost both of his battleships and two of his four destroyers. Another of his destroyers was out of action, and his heavy cruiser was damaged. Shima's force of three cruisers and four destroyers entered Surigao Strait about 0325 when a PT boat put a torpedo into his light cruiser, the *Abukuma*. By 0325, Nishimura's force was already badly mauled, and in the confusion of the retreat of the two fleets, the cruiser *Nachi*, which was the flagship of Shima's fleet, steered close across the bow of the *Mogami*; the two collided at 0430, further damaging the *Mogami* and limiting the speed of the *Nachi* because of damage to her stern.

Our arriving planes found the remnants of the Nishimura-Shima fleets in flight toward the west. These ships were by then receiving some protection from shore-based Japanese fighters. The torpedo planes fought their way through intercepting Japanese aircraft and heavy antiaircraft fire to drop their torpedoes. Later, after returning to the ship, aircrews reported observation of four hits out of six drops on what was believed to be a *Kongo*- or *Fuso*-class battleship in addition to bomb hits on other ships by the fighters. The only battleships in these two fleets were the *Yamashiro* and the *Fuso*. Records of the battle now indicate that the *Yamashiro* went to the bottom at 0419 and the *Fuso* blew apart and sank in two halves at 0430. As with many battles, there is some confusion, but the composite evidence is that Butch Vincent's attack finished the already-damaged *Fuso*. Nishimura's destroyer, *Asagumo*, which was then out of action, was later sunk at 0721 by the American cruisers *Denver* and *Columbia*.

The *Suwannee* carried only nine torpedoes in her magazine, and the VT planes in Butch Vincent's flight had expended four of them. A later flight that was led by Bob Chase against Kurita's force in the north also carried and expended four. Jimmie Dunn, on a still later flight, carried the ninth and last torpedo. Radioman Bob Smith later related while at NAS Daytona Beach that he had ridden through three torpedo attacks that day, which means that Bob was with Vincent's flight, Chase's flight, and Dunn. Thus,

Vincent's flight must have returned to the *Suwannee* before she was temporarily out of action near 0740. This is consistent with the *Suwannee* landing a returning flight near 0730 and supports the conclusion that Vincent's flight hit the *Fuso*. Certainly Vincent's flight could have been in the Surigao area on or before 0430, but the landing near 0730 makes impossible their presence in the Surigao area as late as 0710 when the *Asagumo* went down and unthinkable that the flight was anywhere near the area when the heavy cruiser *Mogami* was severely damaged at 0910 by CVE aircraft. (The *Mogami's* crew was later taken off by a Japanese destroyer, which finished the *Mogami* with a torpedo.) The only other ship in the combined Nishimura-Shima force that was sunk was the damaged light cruiser *Abukuma*, and she was dispatched the next day by land-based U.S. Army bombers. The conclusion is that Vincent's attack must truly have been on one of Nishimura's two battleships, the *Fuso*, and not on a cruiser.

The northernmost group of CVEs at Surigao Strait, Taffy 3, came under attack by Kurita's force with the mighty *Yamato's* guns opening fire at 0649 at a range of nearly 20 miles. Armed aircraft aboard the *Suwannee* were launched as soon as possible, but this was not immediate because the *Suwannee* herself came under attack. Taffy 1 came under kamikaze attack shortly after bogeys were picked up at 0738 on the radar. Four planes soon appeared overhead. The first, a Zeke, dove at 0740 and impacted the *Santee*, and 30 seconds later a second Zeke made a dive on the *Sangamon* but was blown apart by a direct hit from one of the *Suwannee's* five-inch guns. A third Zeke dove on the *Petrof Bay*, but due to heavy antiaircraft fire in combination with the pilot's limited flight experience, the pilot hit alongside the ship. During the confusion, a Japanese submarine, the *I-56*, managed to get close enough to fire a spread of torpedoes at the *Santee*, and one actually hit. However, it was either a glancing impact or the submarine was too close for the torpedo to fully arm, because it bounced off the hull and exploded close alongside. Damage to the *Santee* was relatively light but was sufficient to allow enough water to enter the hull to produce a list of six degrees. However, the *Santee* was operational by 0900.

The fourth kamikaze, still in the air at this time, had apparently been hiding in the blind cone of the radar directly above the *Suwannee*. It was spotted visually near 0800 and rolled over into a steep dive. Though hit by antiaircraft fire during its dive, this plane, a Judy, impacted the *Suwannee* about 40 feet forward of the after elevator. It penetrated through the flight deck, leaving the front silhouette of an airplane — a round hole from the engine and slits from the wings. It also penetrated to the hangar deck where its

The first hole in the *Suwannee's* flight deck.

A portion of the hangar deck after the first kamikaze impact.

The patch over the first hole.

bomb exploded; the plane's wreckage wound up on the main deck. The damage on the hangar deck was extensive, with an unserviceable TBM being set on fire. Casualties were high. The number of injured overflowed the sick bay and required the officers' wardroom to be converted into an auxiliary sick bay. Frog La Fargue and Lip Singleton were on the flight deck at the time of the attack; Frog was by the island while Lip was walking aft. When the antiaircraft fire began, they looked up and saw the diving plane. Lip reversed direction and sprinted for the bow while Frog leaped into the catwalk. Had the Judy not penetrated the flight deck before exploding, both would have been casualties.

It took some gallant effort, but the fire was put out in a relatively short time. This was followed by a diligent expenditure of energy to repair and return the ship to operational status, which was accomplished in stages between 0930 and 1030. This first hole in the flight deck through which the Judy had penetrated had been patched with a one-eighth-inch metal patch. Damage to the hydraulic systems had taken the after elevator out of service and had made all but the aft two arresting wires unserviceable. Luckily, the elevator was in the raised position, but loss of all but the two aftermost arresting wires made for a very restricted landing area.

The kamikaze attack had resulted in an inoperative period of only slightly more than two hours. Strikes against Kurita's force were launched as soon as possible, with the first including four TBMs loaded with torpedoes. It was led by Bob Chase and included Walter Truslow, Gene Sabin, Tim Casey, and their crews. Based on statements by Herbie Beckerdite, it seems that in the turmoil of the repairs and the haste to launch this early strike, time was not available to load bombs on all the *Suwannee* fighters. Beckerdite related that his division made only diversionary strafing attacks. He also intimated that 50-caliber slugs were about as effective on a battleship or cruiser as rain on a well-maintained roof.

Kurita still had a formidable force, though it had by then been reduced from its original strength by the loss of its *Maya* and *Atago* cruisers to our submarines *Dace* and *Darter* on 23 October, while transiting the Palawan passage, as well as the loss of its battleship *Musashi* to air attack by planes of Halsey's Task Force 38 on 24 October, while passing through the Sibuyan Sea. At the initiation of the Battle off Samar, Kurita's force had consisted of 4 battleships, 10 cruisers, and 15 destroyers. In comparison, Ziggy Sprague's Taffy 3 with six *Casablanca*-class carriers carrying one five-inch gun each and a screen of three destroyers and four destroyer escorts was not a very powerful force. But our VT boys and the accompanying fighters gave a good account of themselves. The VT dropped their loads with two torpedo hits and a probable being reported. One of the hits was by Tim Casey on the *Yamato*, the most heavily armed battleship afloat.

The combination of the air attacks by the CVE planes and the gallant efforts by Taffy 3's screening destroyers and destroyer escorts resulted in torpedo hits on the cruisers *Chokai*, *Chikuma*, and *Kumano* as well as bomb damage to the cruiser *Suzuya*. The *Chokai* and *Chikuma* were both rather badly crippled by 0900 and both later went to the bottom. In return, the Japanese shelling was not without effect. The CVE *Gambier Bay* was sunk at 0907, and from the screen the destroyers *Hoel* and *Johnston* and the destroyer escort *Samuel B. Roberts* were lost. At 0923 Kurita gave the order to his ships to regroup and retire to the north. One can understand his confusion. He had mistaken Taffy 3's CVEs for considerably faster CVL carriers. There were more planes overhead than could have come solely from Taffy 3, which was probably rationalized as more "fleet" carriers to the southeast, because at 0810 the battleship *Haruna* had reported a distant sighting of a second carrier group in that direction. This was undoubtedly Stump's Taffy 2. Furthermore, Kurita knew that Nishimura had been engaged by a fleet in Surigao Strait, but communication was poor and he had received little detail. Plain-language radio transmissions between Ziggy Sprague and the command center in Leyte Gulf gave information that there was a battle fleet to the south that could come to the aid of Taffy 3 in approximately two hours. With this mix of information and without shore-based air protection to cover his fleet, Kurita obviously considered it imprudent to stay. The Japanese destroyer *Nowacki* was apparently lost to the CVE plane strikes as she lagged behind Kurita's retreating fleet to assist one of the crippled cruisers. The already-damaged *Suzuya* was also lost when she was again pummeled by American aircraft at 1010, and after a fire that was started during the attack had reached her torpedoes, she was abandoned and sank.

Later a call came to make a strike on a cruiser and a destroyer on the west side of Samar in the Visayan Sea. At that time, these two ships were believed to be survivors of the Surigao Strait battle. In actuality, they were not part of any of the four Japanese battle forces but were heading south on an odd transport mission (Hoyt, 321). A total of 23 Avengers and 19 fighters were on the strike. These included from the *Suwannee:* Jimmie Dunn, Geltchy Golsh, and Bob Chase in TBMs and Fish Fischer, Eggbert Barber, Frog La Fargue, and others in F6Fs. VT 60's Jimmie Dunn carried the *Suwannee's* only remaining torpedo. Several bomb hits were reported, and Dunn's torpedo was a hit. The cruiser, the *Kinu*, and the destroyer, the *Uranami*, were badly damaged, and both sank the next day. During the later part of the attack on these two ships, the American planes were jumped by some Zekes. Hubert "Blackie" Cornwell later reported hearing Frog's voice on the radio saying, "Well, what do you know. I finally got one of the son of a bitches!"

The three torpedo attacks in which VT 60's Bob Smith participated are in marked contrast to those of VT 8's crews, who were all lost during their torpedo attacks at the Battle of Midway in June 1942. One difference was that VT 60 was flying TBMs rather than the TBDs (Douglas Devastators) of VT 8. More importantly, during VT 60's attacks there was coordinated air support from other aircraft; this was absent for VT 8 at Midway. The Japanese commented on the fierceness with which American CVE pilots fought on 25 October. Kurita's operations officer noted, "The bombers and torpedo planes were very aggressive and skillful, and the coordination was impressive."

On that morning of 25 October, CarDiv 22 earned the dubious distinction of being the first carrier division to come under kamikaze attack, with the *Santee* and the *Suwannee* being number one and number two among the many carriers to suffer kamikaze damage during World War II. A minimal accounting of casualties that day was reported in the *Suwannee's* action report, which stated that 5 officers and 80 enlisted men were known dead, 13 officers and 89 enlisted men were injured, and 2 officers and 56 enlisted men were missing in action. This was an initial and cursory tally and was undoubtedly too low. A later and more reasonable estimate indicated close to 100 fatalities and about the same number wounded. But within two hours of the attacks, both the *Santee* and the *Suwannee* were again capable of launching and recovering aircraft. The *Suwannee* operated through the remainder of 25 October and the morning of the 26th without accident, even though the ship had only limited capacities. Bob Misbach, LSO, deserves the lion's share of credit for the way that he managed the landing aircraft, but the skill of the pilots must also be acknowledged. Following the kamikaze attack on the ship, the operational use of only the aftermost two wires would have meant that the inbound aircraft had to land within a space of roughly 50 feet. If the third wire was truly functional, as some believe, this would have extended the latitude to only about 70 feet. In either case, the accomplishment is a reflection of a skillful cooperation between LSO and pilots.

Resumed operations had allowed Taffy 1 to recover planes from earlier flights and, after rearming, launch them on strikes toward Kurita's retiring force. However, after Kurita's departure and before the return of the *Suwannee* to operational status, Taffy 3 had come under air attack and lost the carrier *St. Lo* to kamikazes by 1135; she became the first American ship to be sunk by kamikazes. Indeed, between Kurita's attack and the air strikes, Taffy 3's remaining four carriers all had some damage, and several other vessels in the screen had been hit. The later air strikes that were sent north in pursuit of Kurita carried bombs both on the F6Fs and in the TBMs. Strikes continued to be launched in pursuit of Kurita's retiring force with the last strike of that day by the *Suwannee* departing the ship at 1530. These strikes put Kurita's ships under attack several times, with the last occurring in or near the San Bernardino Strait at the northern tip of Samar. A number of bomb hits were credited to Air Group 60 pilots, but the actions were so extensive that credit to individual pilots is hard to assign.

That last strike involved flight over the greatest distance and put Kurita under attack between 1700 and 1800. Several bomb hits were scored, including hits by Blackie Cornwell and John "Rich" Richardson. (Rich and Ralph "Ash" Ashbridge had joined the squadron just before departure from Sea Adler Harbor for the Philippines as replacement pilots for Slim Bannister and Charlie Lamb.) By the time this strike was completed, planes were already low on gas. They headed for Tacloban airstrip on Leyte. En route, Rich and Blackie were wingmen, respectively, for William "Hank" Keil and Cess Wilson. They encountered four Lilys and accounted for two, one by Hank and one by Blackie. This consumed more gas. Unfortunately, Rich had not yet learned the nuances of being miserly with one's fuel, and en route to Tacloban, while over Samar, he exhausted his supply. He survived his forced landing on that island and was later recovered but returned to the squadron only after it was back in the States. The rest of the planes made it to Tacloban.

Planes from the *Kinu* attack also had landed there, but it was so late that flare pots were laid along the sides of the runway. According to Frog, the flare pots in combination with the soft ground made those landings a memorable experience. All of the pilots in those flights spent the night at Tacloban in something less than luxurious comfort. Those pilots whose planes were still operational flew missions early in the morning and landed back aboard by midmorning.

While the CVEs were busy with the Nishimura, Shima, and Kurita fleets, Halsey's CVs and CVLs were busy with Ozawa's fleet. Halsey had lost the CVL *Princeton* on 24 October to land-based army bombers while his planes were busy in the Sibuyan Sea sinking Kurita's battleship *Musashi*. Halsey's force then had moved north in pursuit of Ozawa's ships; this had left the San Bernardino Strait unguarded to allow Kurita's exit to the east into the expanse of the Pacific. On 25 October, Halsey's carriers launched a total of five strikes spread throughout the day, with the first arriving over the Japanese fleet shortly after 0800 and the last between 1700 and 1800. Halsey's planes sank all four of Ozawa's carriers and one destroyer. At the time of contact, the number of planes aboard the Japanese carriers must have been no more than 71 aircraft. The American force had overwhelming numerical superiority.

While all this other activity was in progress, we VF 60 pilots who had landed at Tacloban in the late morning or early afternoon of 25 October had managed to scrounge ammunition for our guns and fuel for the planes that were still operational. We also managed to obtain something to eat. A young Navy lieutenant who later received a Navy Cross for his efforts organized radio control for aircraft operation and coordinated activities on the ground. He scheduled aircraft back into the air as they became available with mission depending upon immediate need.

Dew Timm and I were scheduled with two other *Suwannee* pilots to go on a routine patrol. This patrol was completed late in the afternoon, and we headed back to the carrier. After arrival at Taffy 1 and landing aboard, we found out how badly the *Suwannee* had been hit. The metal roller doors on the side of the hangar deck had been in the open position for ventilation, and these closures were jammed. There were also large and jagged blast holes exposing the hangar deck to the outside world. The bulkhead aft of the elevator was perforated; this was the forward bulkhead of our sleeping quarters. In these quarters, the two desks that had been attached to the bulkhead had been blown across the room against the lockers on the far side, causing light to leak from the room through the bulkhead perforations and through the openings on the hangar deck to the outside world. Blackout at night meant that no light could be turned on in the room when it was dark outside. Debris on the hangar deck was still scattered about, and the stench of burnt flesh there was nauseating. Almost everyone traveled fore and aft via the catwalks in the open air.

Upon returning to the *Suwannee* that day, I did not know that this, my 103rd landing, with only two arresting cables, was to be my last aboard the ship. I was surprised when a number of people shook my hand, offered congratulations, and said they were glad to see me back aboard. I initially thought this was because I had just bagged my first Zeke, but that seemed strange because everyone was scoring. It turned out to be a case of confusion. One of the flights that had returned earlier to the ship had apparently picked up my radio transmission when I told Dew of a rough engine. Only a short time later another transmission came from a plane going into the water west of Leyte. When the *Suwannee* flight had returned, they had passed the word that I had gone swimming in Ormoc Bay. That explained the reactions to seeing me back aboard so quickly! But the misunderstanding was to be fateful, because the belief that I was not aboard led to my being left off the next day's flight schedule. I was then belatedly added to the schedule but was not due to take off until afternoon on 26 October. Absence from the morning flight schedule would result in transformation by the upcoming day's events from a flier to a deck officer.

Chapter 13

Second Hole in the Flight Deck, 26 October 1944

WHEN Dew and I and our roommates went to bed on the evening of 25 October 1944, we remembered that the lights shouldn't be turned on because of the shrapnel holes in the forward bulkhead. We groped around in the dark, finding our berths. On the way, I hit my shins against my desk, which had been ripped off the bulkhead and moved to the new location during the kamikaze attack. The next morning, when the early flights were taking off for their assigned missions, I got up for breakfast, remembering to take care to avoid the overturned desk.

Normally, pilots ate in the ward room, but because it had been converted to an auxiliary sick bay, the food and utensils were available at the galley door, to be carried up the ladder to the ready room where we could eat. When finished, we returned the cup, plate, and silverware to the galley. After breakfast, I proceeded to the hangar deck for a firsthand look at the damage — it was worse than I thought. The place was a shambles with wrecked air-planes and debris scattered at random. Even with a fresh breeze coming in through jammed roller doors and blast punctures, the stench of death was not conducive to long visits.

I returned to my room, and because it was daylight outside, I could use the lights. I lifted my desk to its upright position and moved it back against the bulkhead, though unsecured. I checked my seashell collection and found that a large fraction had been broken, as had the glass in the frame with my girlfriend's picture. One of the perforations in the bulkhead was located such that, had I been sitting upright in my bunk, the blast fragment would have caught me about belt-high. However, in wartime, "close" and "maybe" don't amount to much. When I finished straightening the room I went to see what help I could be elsewhere, before my scheduled afternoon flight. There was no trouble keeping busy; there were plenty of ways to be useful. Shortly before noon, those of us who were scheduled for the early afternoon launch got into our flight gear, proceeded by the galley to get lunch, and again went to the ready room to eat. The stewards had outdone themselves; in an attempt to boost morale, they had prepared fried chicken.

Frog, Blackie, Eggbert, and Ash, after spending the night at Tacloban, had managed to obtain Army gasoline and ammunition and had flown a morning CAP there before returning to the *Suwannee*. Their four fighters with three others were forward on the flight deck. The ship was turned into the wind and was taking aboard TBMs that were returning from a morning launch. Two were aboard and had been spotted; a third had just landed and was taxiing forward. A few more planes were on the forward portion of the hangar deck, already fueled, and several of these had been armed. Then, the sound of antiaircraft fire came unexpectedly from the carrier's guns. A fraction of a second later, the squawk box was sounding the bugle for "general quarters," but the words, "General quarters! General quarters! All hands man your battle stations," were not yet completed when there was a tremendous explosion. It was the sort of thing that you don't really hear but rather feel as your chest heaves in and out from the differential pressure passing by. We were stunned and surprised, but my most vivid memory is of pieces of fried chicken flying through the air as people bolted from their seats to proceed to battle stations. Incoming kamikazes had not been detected by radar because they had trailed closely behind the returning flight and were mistaken, therefore, as friendly. Everyone streamed from the ready room and up to the flight deck.

A second, less violent explosion was heard by the time we had gained the passageway. Upon reaching the flight deck, we found that beyond the forward elevator it was completely obscured by smoke. The nearest fire hose was just outside the ready room, so several of the group ran back down the ladder to break it out. It was pulled back up to the flight deck, and a crewman was left to turn it on when he got the word to do so. By the time the others returned to the flight deck they were stringing out the hose toward the bow; other groups were doing the same thing with hoses from various parts of the ship. Fortunately, the engine room on a tanker is toward the aftermost part of the hull, so that power generation was not lost and there was plenty of water pressure.

The wounded that could be reached on the deck were placed on stretchers and taken to sick bay. Sporadic antiaircraft fire continued for some time, interspersed with similar sounds from exploding rounds of 50-caliber ammunition aboard the burning airplanes. Fortunately, none of the depth charges in the TBMs exploded. How much of this later antiaircraft fire was directed at enemy planes and how much of it was simply nervousness on the part of the gunners is unknown. There was later a tale about a gunner on one of the two quadruple 40-millimeter mounts on the stern of the ship who was said to have opened fire on some poor pilot who had just been catapulted from a carrier astern of the *Suwannee*. The rumor also stated, however, that some cooler head had physically knocked the man away from the trigger.

Water continued to be poured onto the fire that was eating away the forward flight deck but without effect, due to the forced draft over the fire from the ship's speed. The bridge had been severely damaged. Several there had been killed, including the air officer and the navigator. Others, including the captain, were wounded. Some personnel on the bridge were either blown or jumped over the side. The flight deck crew also suffered the same diversity of casualties. The officers' quarters forward of the hangar deck and CIC (Combat Intelligence Center) were hard hit and, like the bridge and flight deck, suffered many casualties.

Though bleeding badly from shrapnel wounds, the captain remained on deck and encouraged those involved in fighting the fires. The bridge on the island had been gutted and thus the conn had been moved to the aft starboard catwalk, from where the engines were ordered stopped, and the ship decelerated to become dead in the water. As a result, the flow of air across the deck was reduced and the fire fighting became more effective. Under these circumstances, "fortunate" may be an inappropriate word, but two factors worked in our favor. First, all Japanese aircraft had by then departed the scene, so that air attack was no threat. Second, we stopped directly over the spot that one of the destroyers had just reported a submarine contact. A torpedo shot by a submarine directly below a ship is difficult and even if accomplished endangers the submarine itself. Thus, no attack came while

The next four pictures are a sequence showing the second kamikaze (circled) progressing through its dive until impact on the USS *Suwannee* (in background on subsequent photos) on 26 October 1944. The TBM pilot flying by the ship is Rex "Arkie" Paul, who was part of the returning TBM flight. (National Archives)

The *Suwannee*, dead in the water and down by the bow. (National Archives)

the ship was dead in the water and completely vulnerable.

The kamikaze had impacted atop the taxiing TBM just after it had crossed the barriers onto the forward elevator. The explosion had annihilated the TBM and its crew of Fred "Bugs" Beidelman, radioman Frank Barnard, and gunner Arnold Delmenico. The elevator itself was bent into a V-shape and blown to the bottom of its well. An I-beam of four or five feet high that had supported the flight deck just forward of the elevator was severely twisted into an odd configuration. Aircraft on the forward end of the flight deck were leaking gasoline into the elevator well, onto the forecastle, and into the catwalks, causing the fire to spread. The fire in the elevator well was particularly dangerous to the ship's survival, because aircraft that were down on the hangar deck were already fueled and some already loaded with ordnance for the afternoon flights. However, the damaged shape of the elevator helped to channel the draining gasoline to contain the fire until Chief William Brooks bravely managed to get to the valves that activated the hangar deck sprinkler system.

Many of our ordnancemen and plane handlers who had been on the forward flight deck performing their assigned tasks had been killed outright. Others in the catwalks had been burned, some fatally, by the leaking gasoline; ultimately, many had been forced to go over the side. People in the forward portion of the ship found it impossible to move aft, and many fled to the bow. The situation on the forecastle became impossible when the metal deck and rail became too hot to touch. Robert "Chief" Nesbitt had been in forward officers' country and found himself forced into this position. With the increasing heat, there remained no alternative but to abandon ship. Chief described his departure as "making like a monkey" down the anchor chain and, after hanging from the anchor, dropping into the water. He was later picked up with others by one of the screening destroyers.

After what seemed an interminable time, the fire began to come under control. But so much water had been pumped onto the forward portion of the ship that she was down by the bow some four to six feet. The weaker second explosion that had shortly followed the kamikaze blast had left a large hole in the vicinity of the catapult. Whether this second explosion resulted from the weakening and subsequent rupture of the pressurized air tank that fired the catapult or from a bomb dropped from a second plane is still moot. This second explosion certainly made its contribution to our dead and injured.

As the fires abated, it became possible to get help into some of the areas where casualties were trapped. One of the worst of these was CIC. It was located forward and to the starboard of the impact point of the kamikaze and just one deck below the flight deck. This was where the radars were monitored and where all communications were funneled; coding and decoding equipment was also located there. One of the wounded in CIC was Ivor Thomas, officer in charge of fighter direction and whose talents were respected by all pilots. The space could not be entered until the fire was under control. Smoke density in the area was particularly heavy. Corky Finley was one of several who donned breathing apparatus to repeatedly enter this smoke-filled area to rescue wounded and trapped personnel who would otherwise have perished. He and other individuals all earned medals for their bravery in penetrating this dangerous space of restricted visibility with its maze of jagged protrusions, displaced furnishings and equipment, and distorted decks and bulkheads. The selfless performance of the entire crew on both the 25th and 26th cannot be commended too highly.

Once the fire was under reasonable control, the ship could again get underway. It was conned from the jury bridge that had been rigged on the port side in the catwalk just forward of the landing signal officer's station. The ship was capable of undertaking evasive maneuvers, and its motion through the water felt comforting. However, as an operational aircraft carrier, it was obvious that the *Suwannee* was out of business. All aircraft that were aboard on the forward end of the flight deck were junk, and those below on the hangar deck couldn't be raised to the flight deck, even if any could be salvaged. In addition, the requisite numbers and specialties of personnel for flight operations were inadequate. *Suwannee* aircraft still in the air were forced to divert to other carriers that remained operational.

Out of a complement of approximately 1,100 officers and men, it has been estimated that the number of fully functional personnel aboard the *Suwannee* by the evening of 26 October was between 150 to 250. The accuracy of that estimate may be questioned, but there is no doubt the number was well below 50 percent of the allotted complement. Official records show that on the two days of 25 and 26 October, fatal casualties totaled 267, and the number of wounded must have been at least comparable. Many had been scattered here and there: some had gone over the side and were either lost in the water or picked up by other ships, and some of the flight crews had been stranded on the beach or had landed on other ships. Further impairing our operational capability, the flight deck forward of the bridge was charcoal, and the catapult was no longer functional.

It took a long time to collect all of the scattered and surviving members of the crew, with many stragglers not getting back aboard until after the ship had returned to Sea Adler Harbor. The *Suwannee's* condition made her more of a liability than an asset to Taffy 1. She was therefore detached back to Palau (then in American hands) to offload wounded and proceed on to the Admiralties to rendezvous with the fleet after their release from duty in the Philippines.

The *Suwannee* departed Taffy 1 at 0205 on 27 October. The destroyer escort USS *Coolbaugh* was assigned to shepherd her south. Nerves among the *Suwannee's* crew were very taut. The ship was hardly beyond sight of the carrier division in the early dawn when someone on board shouted, "Submarine!" The destroyer escort plowed along with no indication of a contact, but word of mouth flew back along the deck to the jury bridge, and the helm was put hard over to port. It turned out that the sighting was actually a porpoise, but the rapidity of the response without verification indicated the still-present tension.

But in spite of this tension, the crew worked together. Rank didn't mean much at that time. Aircrews took over ship's company watches. We pilots, when standing bridge watches, must have given the old salts a real chuckle, because we knew little about ship handling; many of us made fools of ourselves. The pilots also did some of the navigation. Charles "Freddie the Ferret" Frederick was an administrative officer in VF 60 who had taught celestial navigation at a VP (patrol plane) training base. He replaced Lieutenant Premo, the ship's navigator, and he allowed pilots to try their hand at what was for them a very different kind of navigation. Tex Garner described the operation as the blind leading the blind. A group of three pilots would each take a set of star sights and fix the ship's position. These fixes would be plotted and would seldom or never agree, so the men compromised by choosing the mean of the three positions. In any case, and with Freddie's help, they managed to make landfall on four different occasions without putting the ship aground on some godforsaken reef.

A word about Freddie is in order. During normal operations at sea, he was not kept particularly busy and, therefore, took a bit of friendly ribbing from the pilots. However, during this period of crisis, he was a stalwart pillar who anticipated things that needed to be done and efficiently managed to solve problems as they arose.

When off watch and not occupied with ship's business there was still plenty to do, and all hands worked together. The ship had to be cleaned up. Junk and debris were thrown over the side. Onerous jobs were partitioned equally. Able-bodied helped the incapacitated with simple chores such as washing and eating. All contributed in some way. The dead were treated with respect. Each corpse was securely wrapped in canvas, and six firebricks were placed in one-two-three sequence between the legs to weight the body for burial at sea. A dog tag was taken from each body so that the records could be kept and relatives could be notified. One burned seaman in particular sticks indelibly in memory. When he was rolled over onto the canvas, the movement caused a belch. It is my fervent hope never to smell anything like that again; some lost their lunch. The corpse was not recognizable, but the dog tag indicated that he was one of the ship's young officers who had participated in a very philosophical discussion on the bow of the flight deck only a few evenings before. That was a hard way to be taught the ephemerality of life.

Inventory of the dead shipmates' personal possessions was necessary before these could be sent home. The prime directive was to be sure that nothing would be included that would be offensive to the family or would leave an erroneously negative impression of the departed. Fortunately, as far as is known, no one doing inventories ever ran into anything that he thought would fall into that category. However, it was surprising to see some of the things that people think are worth keeping. By the time that the *Suwannee* reached Palau to offload the wounded onto the hospital ship *Bountiful*, the *Suwannee* was at least free of debris and was clean and presentable. Admittedly, she was far from having the "spit and polish" attendant to an Annapolis inspection and she still reeked of the odoriferous burnt smells, but that was not from our lack of effort.

At Palau, the American troops were still engaged in the mopping-up of scattered Japanese resistance, particularly so on the large island of Babelthuap. When we anchored close to a hospital ship in Kossel Roads, our ship was close enough to the shore of the island that it was conceivable that enemy personnel might paddle out in small craft under cover of darkness to attempt a surreptitious boarding. This perception of danger was not unreasonable in view of the demonstrated suicidal tendencies of Japanese fighting men, and thus small arms were issued aboard the *Suwannee*. While the ship was anchored there a guard was routinely maintained to prevent boarding. Four-hour watches in the dead of night with the weight of a 45-caliber automatic hanging from one's belt was not exciting. But once the wounded had been offloaded onto the hospital ship, *Suwannee* was free to proceed back to the Admiralties to ride the hook. She waited there for the ships of CarDiv 22 to be detached and rejoin her when their work in the Philippines was completed.

On the trip from the Philippines to the Admiralties, pilots had become acquainted with the seagoing duties of a ship's officer, but in the Admiralties they became exposed to duties while in port. Pilots' services for ship's duties remained necessary because, even though most of the able-bodied people who had been picked up by other ships had returned aboard during *Suwannee's* stay in the Admiralties, the number of wounded and fatalities combined with the number still missing had reduced the total complement by roughly 50 percent. None of the pilots was sufficiently experienced to qualify to stand Officer of the Deck watch, but by that time we were experienced enough to hold down the number two position as Junior Officer of the Deck (JOD), albeit somewhat inexpertly in most cases. This meant that when the captain was off the bridge, as he was at that time with his wounds, the JOD was in the number two decision-making position with respect to running the ship. As snot-nosed 21- to 23-year-old kids, the gravity of the responsibility was lost on many.

Responsibilities of the JOD in port differed from the responsibilities when under way at sea. At sea, sufficient repairs had been made to the bridge within a day to make it usable, and the JOD stood his watches there. He monitored the ship's course through the zigzag pattern, monitored the engine revolutions and the ship's speed, relayed the OD's orders to the appropriate division of the ship, and relayed all information and problems from the operating divisions back to the OD, usually being rewarded with the directive, "Take care of it." When in company with other ships, he was involved with "station keeping," keeping position with respect to bearings and distances to other ships in the formation. In port, the JOD stood watch with the OD on the quarterdeck, the boarding area; duties included monitoring boarding and departures from the ship and taking responsibility for seeing that proper recognition was given when merited by a visitor's rank.

Other duties were also assigned to the pilots while in port. Pilots, acting as ship's officers, might be assigned such chores as commanding the whale boat and its crew to run guard mail through the fleet and to shore. Guard mail is the naval equivalent to the interoffice mail of large companies or universities. Or duties of a liaison mission to another vessel in the harbor might be undertaken. Such missions took us aboard a variety of vessels never before seen close up. On one occasion, I boarded a sleek destroyer escort for the first time; I was impressed by the narrow beam and low freeboard amidships. Transiting fore and aft on the deck in a heavy sea must have been a wet experience.

Duty as a ship's officer was a totally new experience for a fighter pilot whose responsibilities had previously been in the air, and those primarily to his wingman and himself. During the initial stages of transition to this new environment, all pilots were inexperienced and totally inept, but necessity leads to rapid progress. By the time the rest of the carrier division had rejoined the *Suwannee* in the Admiralties and she was ready to weigh anchor for Pearl Harbor, most were reasonably comfortable with what they were doing.

Chapter 14

Return Home

SHORTLY after the *Suwannee* reached Sea Adler Harbor in the Admiralties, the ship's first lieutenant, third in command aboard ship, was detached to fly back to the U.S. His destination was the Bremerton Navy Yard on Puget Sound in the state of Washington. He took with him blueprints from the ship's files, as well as pictures and detailed written descriptions of the damage from the two kamikaze pilots. The availability of this material would allow the Bremerton Navy Yard to make an early assessment of the rebuilding task, facilitating rapid repair of the *Suwannee* after her arrival in Puget Sound in late November. All major components (for example, the forward elevator) would be prefabricated while the *Suwannee* was in transit stateside and ready for installation by the time she would dock at the yard.

But before she could reach Puget Sound, the *Suwannee* and the rest of CarDiv 22 had to sail for Pearl Harbor in Hawaii. At Pearl, there was very little that could be done for the *Suwannee*, but she did stay for a couple of days while everything that might be usable in the war effort was offloaded rather than carried back to the States to be reshipped later. While in Pearl, most of the air group got liberty. Corky and I with a couple of other pilots were roaming around together when we decided we would like to see the island. We "borrowed" an unattended government jeep and wandered all over Honolulu, up to the Pali, and to a diversity of other places. We had the vehicle from early afternoon until around ten o'clock that night. The tour of the island was quite extensive; in fact, it is a wonder that the jeep's gas tank didn't run dry. The jeep was abandoned near Pearl City, where the carrier was berthed.

In November 1944, the *Suwannee* sailed from Pearl Harbor to the States with no escort. It was felt that at this late date in the war, the Japanese navy had been hurt to the extent that the probability of encountering a Japanese submarine en route was minimal. However, the ship still maintained a zigzag pattern on the way home. On that trip, members of the air group for the first time had the opportunity to make friends among the ship's company and to see parts of the ship that in normal operations would not be visited. On one occasion, they toured the engine room to see the ship's propulsion apparatus, led by a young engineering officer whose invitation was an expression of his gratitude for help received while recuperating from his burns. He explained how the boilers were fired, how the steam lines were run to the twin turbines, and how each turbine was connected to a screw through a drive shaft.

This latter was particularly impressive because each shaft was 12 inches in diameter. Furthermore, a shaft was not a continuous piece but a series of two-foot sections that were flanged at either end, and the sections were bolted together at the flanges. Spare sections were strategically stored along the hull so that in the event of the shaft being sheared, the failed section could be removed and a replacement section be put quickly into service. The fact that shearing of a 12-inch shaft was even contemplated indicates that the twisting forces between a turbine and a screw must be very high. However, this wasn't the only damage insurance; a variety of other spares were bolted into storage spaces to provide ready access for replacement in case of failure of any critical component of the propulsion system.

There were no decks between the flight deck and the hull and personnel made their way around equipment on gratings and catwalks and up and down on ladders. Admiration for the engineers was further enhanced when it was noted that the hull was sweating due to moisture condensation. There, at the base of the engine room, people were well below the waterline, and the cold Pacific Ocean was only an eighth of an inch away on the other side of the steel hull. The ocean was cooling the hull to produce the condensation. A bomb hit or a torpedo hit in this aft 75 to 100 feet of the carrier would make this area a death trap. Even strafing by 50-caliber ammunition would cause a large influx of water.

While still a day or two from entry into Puget Sound, an unusual incident occurred as one of the VF pilots was standing JOD watch. It was late and very dark with stars obscured by cloud cover, and in the latitudes being traversed, it felt quite cold on the open bridge, particularly so after more than a year in the tropics. Suddenly, a green light streaked into the sky several thousand yards astern and to port of the *Suwannee*. It was either a rocket or a star shell, because it reached far too high to have come from a signal pistol. There was nothing in the communications manual or code book to explain it. The OD figured that it would be foolish for a crippled and unescorted carrier to turn around to investigate, and the JOD had no inclination to question his judgment. Thus the ship proceeded on its way.

On another dark and cold night, one of the pilots was again standing JOD watch. On the bridge all personnel were wearing foul-weather gear because though the bridge had a transparent wind screen, it was otherwise exposed to the elements. The sea was fairly heavy so the ship was pitching quite noticeably, and there was a strong wind on the starboard quarter — the right rear. The JOD noticed that the compass card was swinging several degrees from the desired course, first to one side and then the other. He called down the voice tube to the helmsman, also in the island two decks below, "Helmsman, mind your helm!" He got an "Aye, aye, Sir" in response. He noticed the OD glance his way with a partial grin. A few minutes passed and the OD asked if he had ever taken a trick at the helm of a large vessel. When the JOD answered in the negative, the OD asked if he would like to try it. The JOD jumped at the chance, and the pair climbed down the ladder to the wheelhouse where two helmsmen were taking turns at the wheel. The wheel was about five feet in diameter and its motion controlled a steam-driven donkey engine, which was the motive power for moving the large rudder. The man at the wheel let the JOD take over, and the OD returned to the bridge.

The JOD, still wearing the heavy foul-weather gear, soon worked up a sweat. He quickly found that it took a significant amount of effort to turn the wheel, and he learned why the compass card was oscillating from side to side. A carrier has an exceptionally high freeboard with plenty of surface to react to wind. When the stern was high and the bow low, with the pronounced pitching motion, the wind acted against the stern to swing the heading to starboard. When the bow was high and the stern was low, the wind acted on the bow to cause a turn to port. In principle, judicious timing of rudder corrections would be able to compensate to keep the desired heading. In practice, the JOD found this very difficult to accomplish and did a much poorer job of holding a constant heading than either of the regular helmsmen. It wasn't long before a voice came down the speaking tube saying, "Helmsman, mind your helm!" All the JOD could say in response was, "Aye, aye, Sir," as he heard a soft chuckle at the other end of the tube.

He fought the wheel for another 10 or 15 minutes and by that time was pretty well drained. It was then quite obvious why there were two quartermasters on duty. He gave the wheel back to the helmsmen and thanked them for the opportunity and for their advice. He then climbed back to the bridge where he was met with grins all around. The OD came over and asked if he enjoyed his turn at the wheel. The JOD responded that it was hard work and took some skill, but it was something that not everybody got a chance to try, and he thanked the OD for the opportunity. The OD then explained that the current wind and sea conditions were among the more difficult for a helmsman to handle when trying to maintain a constant heading, thus helping alleviate the JOD's dissatisfaction with his own performance. Needless to say, the JOD found no further reason to caution the helmsman to mind his helm.

At speeds within the *Suwannee's* capability, it takes in excess of ten hours to travel to Seattle from the mouth of the Strait of Juan de Fuca between Washington State and Vancouver Island, British Columbia. It is about 100 miles through the strait before turning south into Puget Sound with more than 50 additional miles before docking in Seattle. The days were short at this time of the year, just before the end of November 1944, and because this run was best made during the daylight hours, the *Suwannee's* course and speed were controlled during the last days of the voyage in order to arrive at the mouth of the strait very early in the morning. Thus, the crew's first view of North American territory after nearly a year at sea was Vancouver Island, the northern shore of the strait. It is difficult to describe the emotional reactions among the crew upon seeing home and safety after the experiences of the past year.

Packing was completed during the day, and the ship docked in Seattle late in the afternoon of 26 November. The mooring lines had barely been tied before dockyard workers had swarmed over the vessel checking the damage and scheduling the repairs. It seemed almost sacrilegious to see all of these strangers prowling about on the *Suwannee*. The affection that a seagoing man develops for his ship is difficult to convey. A manned ship is a live, vibrant thing. Without a crew a ship is a hulk, but with a crew it becomes an entity. The *Suwannee* was a part of every man who served on her. These aliens in Seattle may have been necessary, but they simply did not belong.

Because of the first lieutenant's advanced arrival with the damage report and the ship's blueprints, all major replacement components had already been fabricated. They were to be installed after the ship moved to the Bremerton Yard the next day. Air Group 60 personnel were separated from the ship within an hour of docking in Seattle. They carried their seabags down the gangplank and thence to the end of a very long dock. There they boarded buses to be taken to Sand Point Naval Air Station where quarters were to be during their short stay on the shores of Lake Washington. After being fed and assigned rooms it was well after 9:00 p.m., but because this was our first night ashore, Herbie Beckerdite and I caught a cab and went to town to start a party that lasted on and off for the better part of three days. On our second day ashore, after sleeping late and eating lunch, another single pilot and I decided again to go to town to continue the celebration. On the way to the gate, we passed the Waves' barracks. We looked at each other and decided to go in. I walked up to the little Wave at the reception desk and said, "We're in Air Group 60 and just back stateside. We'd like to meet the two prettiest Waves in the barracks that are off duty this afternoon." This apparently was not standard procedure, because her eyes widened and her jaw dropped. She stammered for a second or two before regaining her composure, then hesitantly said, "Just a minute!" She left and walked back into the barracks. She wasn't gone long, and when she returned she said, "If you'll just have a seat over there, they'll be out in a minute." It turned out to be a great afternoon!

Within three days, orders were cut for new assignments. All pilots in the fighter squadron were given a prolonged period of stateside duty. The skipper, Harvey Feilbach, had an engineering background and was reassigned to the Naval Aircraft Factory to perfect the new gun sight that he had designed. Willie Schmall and Ira "Sonny" Pitcher were assigned to a new squadron, VF 66, that was to test the operational capability of the Navy's first jet, the Ryan Fireball, FR-1. It was an unusual aircraft in that it was a hybrid with a reciprocating engine in the nose and a jet in the tail and could fly on either engine. Its tricycle landing gear was also atypical for the time.

Cess Wilson and Fosdick Walters were assigned to the Training Command in Corpus Christi, Texas, while Lip Singleton, Eggbert Barber, Chief Nesbitt, Rabbi Shea, Frog La Fargue, and I were assigned to the Operational Training Command in Jacksonville, Florida. Memory fails with regard to assignments drawn by Fish Fischer and Pappy Knapp, and the rest of the pilots were to reform VF 60 with a stateside tour to train replacement personnel. In the VT squadron, Bill Keller and Luke MacKay were sent to the Operational Training Command, but I am uncertain of the other VT assignments.

With the breakup of the air group in Seattle, all hands got a 30-day leave. This was a bittersweet time of mixed sadness at the breakup and joy at being back in the States. The air group had logged just shy of 5,000 landings aboard the *Suwannee* with nearly 850 of these landings in July 1944, during the period of heavy operations in the Marianas. From 23 February to 7 June 1944, 1,016 carrier landings had been logged without so much as a barrier crash. From 7 June to 29 July, there were an additional 1,379 carrier landings without mishap. In the overall period of slightly more than a year at sea, the air group logged over 21,500 hours in the air. This averages close to 500 hours per pilot.

The air group was responsible for dropping over 310 tons of bombs, was credited with the destruction of 30 Japanese aircraft in aerial combat, and was officially credited with sinking and damaging surface ships as well as one Japanese submarine. No quantitative evaluation can be made of the group's effectiveness in the destruction of or damage to enemy personnel, supplies, aircraft on the ground, small surface craft, transport, and the like. Also, because of the many units engaged in the overall combat, there is no way of really separating the effectiveness of *Suwannee* aircraft from that of others during their bombing, torpedo, and strafing attacks on Japanese warships during 25 and 26 October in the Battle of Leyte Gulf. Postwar records show which ships were sunk, and it is known that *Suwannee's* aircrews contributed significantly with many claims of direct hits. The air group simply did its best in performing the assigned chores.

The *Suwannee* was back at sea in full operational status in late January 1945, just two months after her arrival. It was an amazingly quick turnaround. Evidently the shipyard workers were as patriotic as the crews. (Certainly, they were paid better.) By early February 1945, the *Suwannee* was underway at sea and brought Air Group 40 aboard on 9 February. She supported the invasion of Okinawa on 1 April and continued supporting operations there until 16 June. Then she supported the last seaborne invasion of the war at Balikpapen, Borneo, in the East Indies between 30 June and 5 July 1945. The ship had supported the first seaborne invasion of the war at Casablanca and the last in Borneo. It is no wonder that Samuel Eliot Morrison in his definitive history of World War II naval warfare refers to her as "Good Old *Suwannee*."

The war in Europe ended on 9 May 1945; the war in Japan ended on 15 August. I was among six instructors from the Operational Training Command's NAS Daytona Beach who, while on detached duty, had completed rocket training at Cape May, New Jersey, on 13 August. At Daytona, planes had shifted from F6Fs to FM2s and then to Curtiss SB2C Helldivers. The last shift was because the syllabus had changed from fighter (VF) training to fighter-bomber (VBF) training. The shift was traceable to Harvey Feilbach's thesis that the fighters could serve adequately in the role of dive bombers and after dropping their bomb load could function effectively as fighters. The operation of the F6Fs aboard the *Sangamons* had proven the validity of his thesis.

We six instructors had been given prior authorization to take a day off after completion of our training to fly wherever we wished before returning to NAS Daytona. Most chose New York City. Two of us managed to take in a ball game and a play, but the most impressive event was the crowd in Times Square on 14 August, the night preceding V-J Day. People were everywhere; after four years of war everyone was ready to celebrate and the crowd had gone wild. The Mardi Gras in New Orleans at its most ribald is tame by comparison. Men in uniform were kissed repeatedly by young ladies whom the servicemen had never seen before nor since. The next day, V-J Day, 15 August, all military bases throughout the country were shut down for a one-day celebration. Only skeleton duty sections were maintained. However, we Daytona instructors had no authorization for more than a one-day delay before returning to Florida, so we had to fly. I had trouble getting both my head and my body into the same cockpit. The trip to Florida was thoroughly miserable.

In postwar years, Truman has been criticized for using such an inhumane weapon, the A-bomb, on Japan. In rebuttal, what is humane about being burned by napalm or hit by a kamikaze, or for that matter any of the myriad ways that one can be mangled or killed in a war? I thought then and think now that the dropping of the bombs on Hiroshima and Nagasaki saved more lives than were lost. Intelligence estimates at the time were that there remained some 500,000 Japanese troops in Manchuria and Japan proper. The determination of the Japanese to fight to the death had been adequately demonstrated during every engagement. Thus, if the Allies had been forced to invade the home islands, the casualty count, both civilian and military, would have been enormous.

The *Suwannee* anchored in Nagasaki harbor on 14 September 1945, approximately a month after the bomb drop. Members of her crew got liberty to see firsthand the devastation produced by the atomic blast. By 15 October the *Suwannee* was in Tokyo Bay and remained there until 25 October. As members of her crew like to say, "She made it all the way."

Epilogue

The Kamikaze Corps

THE kamikaze attacks on 25 October represented the first use of organized suicide planes by the Japanese. However, the damages to the *Santee* and the *Suwannee* shortly after 0700 on that date were relatively minor. Later, however, another group of kamikazes found Taffy 3 fleeing from Kurita's surface attack. Two of the suicide planes were successful in their dives on the *St. Lo*; they sent her to the bottom as the first ship to be sunk by kamikaze attack. The suicide planes remained quite active after the *Suwannee's* departure. The initial activity was in the Philippines but was extended to Formosa, Okinawa, and the home islands of Kyushu, Shikoku, and western Honshu. The first fast carrier, the CV *Intrepid*, was hit on 29 October 1944. The next day, the CV *Franklin* and the CVL *Belleau Wood* were both damaged, with the damage to the *Franklin* being severe.

The activity of the kamikaze units in the Philippines persisted while the Allied forces continued moving through those islands to Luzon. Carriers were the preferred targets, but the kamikazes attacked a wide variety of ships. Japanese claims for the period October 1944 through January 1945 indicated that 37 ships, including 5 CV-class carriers, 1 battleship, and 5 cruisers, were sunk by kamikazes, and 59 ships, including 9 CVs, 2 CVLs, and 1 CVE, were damaged (Inoguchi, Nakajima, and Pineau, 126, 233-240). In contrast, U.S. records show only 16 ships sunk with 2 being CVEs and the rest being destroyers or auxiliary vessels. However, U.S. records show that the number of ships damaged was actually 87 rather than the Japanese claim of 59. The damaged ships included 7 CVs, 2 CVLs, and 13 CVEs. This damage cost the Japanese 378 kamikaze planes and 102 escort planes for a total of 480 aircraft.

A surprisingly high percentage of the kamikaze attacks were unsuccessful. This is at least partly attributable to the inexperience of the pilots, but also to the fact that antiaircraft fire was very effective against them; a diving plane presents a large target moving directly at the gun barrels.

By 8 January 1945, American forces had advanced sufficiently far up the Philippine chain that it was obvious the Japanese position was untenable. Accordingly, Japanese orders were cut moving the kamikaze units north to Formosa. All units had departed the Philippines by 10 January, but suicide attacks as late as 8 January 1945 were made with hits being recorded on both the CVE carriers *Kitkun Bay* and *Kadashan Bay* (Inoguchi, Nakajima, and Pineau, 130).

After the Philippines, the next landings were on Okinawa. The *Suwannee* was repaired in time to participate. Softening-up strikes began in March, and troops were put ashore on 1 April 1945 with fighting persisting into June. The kamikazes again were active, and it was there that they added a new wrinkle in the form of the *okha* manned rocket bomb (which the Americans called *baka*, Japanese for "foolish") with stubby wings. This vehicle was carried on a mother ship, usually a Betty, because of the bomb's very limited fuel supply. When a suitable target was near enough to be within range, the *okha* was released for its suicide attack. Apparently, the advantage was that the *okhas* could be manufactured more rapidly, cheaply, and with more limited expenditure of strategic materials than a conventional airplane.

The first use of these bombs was on 21 March 1944 and was a dismal failure. A flight of 18 Bettys, sixteen loaded with *okha* bombs, were sent with 30 escorting fighters to attack 3 carriers. This attack force was intercepted over 50 miles from its intended targets, and all of the mother planes were forced to jettison their *okha* bombs out of range. Of the 18 Bettys, 15 were shot down, and the other 3, by Japanese report, escaped into cloud but never returned from the flight and were presumed lost. Notwithstanding this initial performance, the *bakas* (*okhas*) did have some success and, in combination with conventionally powered suicide planes, significantly damaged Allied ships.

During the several months of the Okinawa operations, Japanese records show that they had a combined loss of 930 kamikaze and escort aircraft. In contrast, the Allies had 17 ships sunk, including 1 CVE, and 198 ships damaged, including 8 CVs and 4 CVEs. The *Sangamon* was among the CVEs damaged. On 4 May 1945, she was hit by two kamikazes resulting in damage so severe that she was deemed not worth repairing. U.S. records summarize losses due to all kamikaze operations as 34 ships sunk and 288 ships damaged. One CVE is included with the sunk and 16 CVs, 3 CVLs, and 17 CVEs are counted among the damaged.

USS *Suwannee*

At the end of World War II, the *Suwannee* was in Japanese home waters. She and the other *Sangamons* had established a reputation for reliability, versatility, and performance — real "can do" ships. The *Sangamons* had been the models for the *Commencement Bay*-class CVEs, and two of these — the *Block Island* and the *Gilbert Islands* — operated with the *Suwannee* during the Balikpapen invasion on Borneo. The *Block Island* had replaced the *Sangamon* in CarDiv 22 after the *Sangamon* was damaged in May 1945, and the *Gilbert Islands* replaced the *Chenango* in June.

After the signing of the unconditional surrender on 15 August 1945, the majority of the CVEs in the Pacific were assigned to participate in transporting servicemen back to the States. The *Suwannee*, however, was held in reserve in Japanese waters in case pockets of resistance to the peace should appear. By September such resistance no longer seemed to be a threat, and the *Suwannee* was redesignated as a heliocopter carrier and was sent back to the States. On 28 October 1945, she was put into reserve status with the 16th Fleet at the Boston Naval Shipyard. On 8 January 1947, she was decommissioned and was put into a cocoon to anchor with that part of the "mothball fleet" that was riding their hooks in the Boston area.

In 1959, the *Suwannee* was stricken from the Navy list and was sold for reconversion to a tanker. The reconversion plans failed to mature, and in 1961 she was sold to be scrapped and was dismantled in Balboa, Spain, in 1962. She was a gallant lady. For those who served aboard her, she remains alive in their hearts. Nary a man jack of them would doubt that she richly deserves the appellation "Good Old *Suwannee*."

Air Group 60

After Air Group 60 was broken up in Seattle, a portion of it reformed after the men had a period of leave. Those pilots who had been transferred were replaced, primarily with pilots fresh from the training command. The reorganized air group trained for approximately six months in the States. They were then assigned to serve aboard another carrier in the Pacific, but that boarding never occurred; the air group was in Hawaii when the surrender was signed. Some of the pilots were sent back to the States almost immediately for separation. Others were first sent to Saipan before a decision was made to send them back to the States for assignment to new duties. These pilots from Saipan, like the pilots who had earlier separated from the air group in Seattle, continued to serve on active duty for longer or shorter periods of time, but only a small number made a career in the Navy: Rabbi Shea, Lip Singleton, Dash Dashiell, and Doc Phillips. All four of these gentlemen rose to the rank of captain. Rabbi at one time commanded a missile cruiser, the USS *Worden*, and Dash commanded one of the large, modern, canted-deck carriers. Lip had a particularly interesting career; he served as a navigator on a carrier, flew Curtiss SC scout planes off a cruiser, commanded an "all weather" squadron at sea, and qualified to fly almost every modern jet in the Navy carrier inventory during training duty.

Many of the *Suwannee* crew either made a career on active duty or remained in one or another Reserve status. Among the pilots, several served long enough in Reserve units to retire. Herbie Beckerdite served both at NAS Oakland and NAS Los Alamitos. At Los Alamitos he attained command of a Reserve fighter squadron and retired as a commander. Geltchy Golsh also flew at Los Alamitos and commanded a torpedo squadron. Kal Kalal flew in a reserve unit at North Island, San Diego. Blackie Cornwell flew at NAS Glenview and retired as a lieutenant commander. Tex Garner flew at NAS Dallas. Joe Delk stayed in aviation and flew for Eastern Airlines. I was the executive officer of a fighter squadron at NAS Olathe, later flew in a patrol squadron at NAS Minneapolis, and retired as a commander. As of 1994, I believe that Tex and I are the only two who are still active as pilots, albeit now in civil aviation.

During the war, Sonny Pitcher and Willie Schmall were privileged to fly the first Navy jets in the form of the hybrid FR-1s, and after the war, those VF pilots who stayed in the Reserve got to fly the earliest of the Navy's pure jets, specifically the FH-1 Phantom and the FJ-1 Fury. The FH-1 was an ancestor of the F-4 Phantom II of the Vietnam War, and the FJ-1 was the straightwing version of what became the F-86 Sabre Jet of the Korean War.

Blackie was among the group to fly the FH-1, and Herbie and I were among the pilots to fly the FJ-1. Only 62 FH-1s and 33 FJ-1s were built; each FJ-1 was almost unique. When their service life expired, only two FJ-1s were still flyable. No one ever successfully bailed out of one. By today's standards, both the FH-1 and the FJ-1 were severely underpowered. Later jets in the Reserve program included the F9 Panther (straight wing) and Cougar (swept wing) and A4 Skyhawk; the F9 could be taken supersonic in a dive. Flying is wonderful — war is not!

Many years have now passed, and each of the survivors of those fateful October days on the *Suwannee* has developed an overlaying crust of other diverse experiences. However, none has forgotten the gallantry, courage, and selfless sharing of his shipmates during that trying period. When two or more of these old comrades sit down to reminisce, the chasm of time disappears and they are as they were.

Bibliography

THE Aviation History Unit. *The Navy's Air War*, ed. A. R. Buchanan (New York: Harper Bros., undated).

Chesnau, R. *Aircraft Carriers of the World, 1914 to Present* (London: Arms & Armour Press, 1984).

Dacus, W. R., and E. Kitzman. *As We Lived It* (USS *Suwannee* Reunion Association, 1992).

Fahey, James C. *The Ships and Aircraft of the United States Fleet*, War Ed. (New York: Ships and Aircraft, 1942).

Frank, Wolfgang. *The Sea Wolves* (New York: Ballantine Books, 1972).

Hoyt, Edwin P. *The Battle of Leyte Gulf* (Chicago, IL: Playboy Press, 1979).

Inoguchi, Captain Rikihei, Commander Tadashi Nakajima, with Roger Pineau. *The Divine Wind*, Bantam Ed. (Annapolis, MD: Naval Institute Press, 1958; New York: Bantam Books, 1978).

Koenig, William. *Epic Sea Battles* (Hong Kong: Octopus Books, Ltd., 1975).

MacIntyre, Donald. *Leyte Gulf, Armada in the Pacific* (New York:

Ballantine Books, 1970).

Morrison, Samuel Eliot. *History of United States Naval Operations in World War II*, Vol. XIV (Boston: Atlantic-Little Brown, 1962).

Orita, Zenji, with Joseph D. Harrington. *I-Boat Captain* (Canoga Park, CA: Major Books, 1976).

Preston, Anthony. *Aircraft Carriers* (New York: Gallery Books, 1979).

Suwannee Press News, Anniversary Issue, 24 September 1944.

Swanborough, G., and P. M. Bowers. *United States Navy Aircraft since 1911* (New York: Funk & Wagnalls, 1968).

Tillman, B. *Hellcat: The F6F in World War II* (Annapolis, MD: Naval Institute Press, 1979).

U.S. Navy Primary Flight Training Manual (Glenview, IL: Naval Air Training Command, NAS Glenview, 1945).

Y'Blood, William T. *Hunter-Killer* (Annapolis, MD: Naval Institute Press, 1983).

Appendix A

(Data as of November 1944)

Air Group 60 Roster

VF Pilot Name	Radio Call
Ralph W. Ashbridge	Ash
Edgar P. Barber	Eggbert
Herbert F. Beckerdite	Beck
Hubert R. Cornwell	Blackie
Leonard M. De Rose	Mike
Harvey O. Feilbach	Cap
Pardee C. Finley	Corky
Edwin A. Fischer	Fish
Roy C. Garner	Tex
Earl Helwig	Skinhead
Ralph F. Kalal	Kal
William H. Keil	Hank
Donald R. Knapp	Pappy
Quinn D. La Fargue	Frog

VF Pilot Name	Radio Call
Paul W. Lindskog	Big Red
Billie L. McManemin	Mac
Kenneth N. Montgomery	Monty
Robert H. Nesbitt	Chief
Ira B. Pitcher	Sonny
John P. Richardson	Rich
Joseph T. Roderick	Joe
Glenn O. Rynearson	Red
Wilbur A. Schmall	Willie
John D. Shea	Rabbi
Royce A. Singleton	Lip
John F. Smith	Smitty
Dean O. Timm	Dew
Herman A. Walters	Fosdick
Givens C. Wilson	Cesspool

VT Pilot Name	Radio Call
Timothy M. Casey, Jr.	Tim
Robert P. Chase	Bob
Clarence J. Delk	Joe
James P. Dunn	Jim
Paul A. Golsh	Geltchy
William C. Keller	Bill
Frank H. Langdon	Frank
Charles A. Leonard, Jr.	Charley
Freeman P. MacKay, Jr.	Luke
Rex Paul	Arkie
Guy E. Sabin	Sabe
Walter Truslow, Jr.	Ted
Warren C. Vincent	Butch

VT Air Crew

Turret Gunners	Radiomen
John A. Ash AMM2c	Richard L. Abbrecht ARM3c
Leon T. Bingham AOM2c	Frederick A. Anger ARM2c
Howard D. Booz AOM2c	Robert Erlich ARM2c
William B. Garlitz AOM2c	Robert C. Gerson ARM2c

Turret Gunners
Ralph D. Hennings AOM1c
Donald E. Huston AOM1c
Dean V. Kopren AOM1c
Harold A. Lurie AMM1c
Jesse H. Melton AMM2c
Donald W. Stoker AOM2c

Radiomen
James E. Goggin ARM1c
Charles W. Herin ART1c
John W. Lee ARM3c
Stewart A. Neasham ARM3c
Robert L. Pinkston ARM3c
Robert W. Smith ARM2c

Support Personnel

Charles L. Frederick, Administrative Executive Officer
Robert Q. Misbach, Landing Signal Officer
Philip B. Phillips, Flight Surgeon
Howard E. Richmond, Air Combat Intelligence Officer
John H. Shanklin, Gunnery Officer

VF 60 Crew

Ernest Dukeheart AMM1c
William C. Humphrey ACRM, Leading Chief
Maxwell L. Madoche YM1c, Air Group Yeoman
Robert N. McCord AOM1c
William H. McManes AEM1c
Chester D. Nickey ACMM, Engineering Chief
Paul B. Reinders ART1c

VT 60 Crew

Clifford N. Barr ACEM
Max R. Bedford AOM1c
John W. Sousley ACMM, Leading Chief
Robert H. Stagg AOM1c
Robert E. Stanley AMM1c
Francis L. Thill PR1c, Parachute Rigger
Thomas G. Wayson AMM1c, Log Yeoman
Chester E. Zieneski ACMM, Engineering Chief

VF 60

VT 60

Roll of Men Who Served in Air Group 60 and Were Transferred

Glenn Abel AMM2c
Joseph Alferio ARM3c
Lieutenant Stanley Anderson
Ensign Josiah Bacon
Ensign Glen Banks
Leonard Beavers, Navy Field Engineer
Clyde Begley ARM3c
Ensign Ivan Beisel
Ensign F. A. Biancha
Ensign R. E. Bordelon
Lieutenant R. L. Border
Ottawa Breedlove, Y1c
Ensign H. H. Brock
Conly Brooks ARM3c
Machinist James Brown
Max Bruce AEM2c
George Bryan ARM3c
Ensign Carroll Bryant
Lieutenant Henry Carey
Martin Carmody ARM3c
Ensign John Cooke
Walter Crider ARM3c
Ensign I. N. Donahue
Jimmy Dunn ARM3c
Lieutenant Commander Allan E. Edmands
Everett Ellison ARM2c
Ralph Foster AMM1c
Ensign D. G. Futrell
Ensign Winston Gunnels
Lieutenant (jg) William Harrington
Stanley Hatwick AOM2c
Charles Henderson ARM3c
Donald Hughes AOM2c
Ensign Harold Jedlund
Ensign Hugh Johnson
James Johnson ARM3c
Ensign W. C. Johnson
Ensign J. H. Lankford
Ensign Justin Lavin
Ensign Eugene Lee
Ensign W. Martin
Harold Massey, S1c
Ensign A. L. Matteson
Ensign J. E. McAtee
Ensign Kenneth McCubbins
Lieutenant (jg) Bascomb Montgomery
Carpenter Harold Neumann
Ensign Walter Nielson
Lieutenant Willard Olson
Lieutenant (jg) Warren Pellett
Lieutenant Commander J. H. Pennoyer
Milton Phillips ARM3c
Ensign Wallace Rowland
Lieutenant Randolph Scott
Thomas Simpson ARM3c
Ensign W. M. Swayne
George Telarski AEM2c
Lieutenant (jg) P. E. Te Pas
Lieutenant (jg) John Tipton
James Tolar ARM3c
Robert Vaughan ARM3c
Lieutenant (jg) Green Wertenbaker
Lieutenant (jg) R. F. Wolf
Lieutenant (jg) Roscoe Zierlein

Appendix B

Records Aboard Ship

October 1943 to October 1944

Takeoffs (March-October 1944)

VF Catapult	1,830
Free Run	302
	2,132
VT Catapult	981
Free Run	30
	1,011
Air Group Total	3,143

Air Group 60 in November 1944 on the way home from the combat area. Each flag represents one Japanese aircraft shot down during aerial combat and each bomb represents five tons delivered by the air group on Japanese targets.

Landings

VF — 2,170 (since 3/15/44)
3,001 (since 10/18/43)

VT — 1,032 (since 3/15/44)

VC — 1,562 (since 10/18/43)

Air Group Total 3,202 (since 3/15/44)
4,563 (since 10/18/43)

Month of most landings:
July 1944
VF - 590
VT - 256
____
846

Consecutive Landings Without Deck Accident

23 February-7 June 1944
1,016

7 June-29 July 1944
1,379

Air Group Flight Time

VF — 10,547.1 hours
VT — 9,311.9 hours
VSB — 1,709.8 hours
____
21,568.8 hours

Month of most hours:
July 1944
VF — 2,040.7 hours
VT — 973.1 hours
____
3,013.8 hours

Ship's Landings Milestones

2,000 — Lieutenant Commander H. O. Feilbach — F6F-3
3,000 — Ensign J. Cooke — SBD-5
4,000 — Ensign J. Roderick — F6F-3
5,000 — Lieutenant (jg) G. E. Sabin — TBM-1c
6,000 — Ensign I. Pitcher — F6F-3

Index

by Lori L. Daniel